CLOUDS OVER
QINGCHENG
MOUNTAIN

by the same author

Climbing the Steps to Qingcheng Mountain
A Practical Guide to the Path of Daoist Meditation and Qigong
Wang Yun
ISBN 978 1 78775 076 0
eISBN 978 1 78775 077 7

of related interest

White Moon on the Mountain Peak
The Alchemical Firing Process of Nei Dan
Damo Mitchell
Foreword by Jason Gregory
ISBN 978 1 84819 256 0
eISBN 978 0 85701 203 6

Heavenly Streams
Meridian Theory in Nei Gong
Damo Mitchell
ISBN 978 1 84819 116 7
eISBN 978 0 85701 092 6

A Comprehensive Guide to Daoist Nei Gong
Damo Mitchell
Foreword by Paul Mitchell
ISBN 978 1 84819 410 6
eISBN 978 0 85701 372 9

Vital Breath of the Dao
Chinese Shamanic Tiger Qigong – Laohu Gong
Master Zhongxian Wu
ISBN 978 1 84819 000 9
eISBN 978 0 85701 110 7

CLOUDS OVER QINGCHENG MOUNTAIN

A Practice Guide to Daoist Health Cultivation

WANG YUN

SINGING DRAGON
LONDON AND PHILADELPHIA

First published in Great Britain in 2021 by Singing Dragon,
an imprint of Jessica Kingsley Publishers

An Hachette Company

1

Copyright © Wang Yun 2021
Translated by the Modern Wisdom Translation Group

Front cover image source: Shutterstock®.

Disclaimer: The practice of *qigong* is intended to be a complementary therapeutic practice, its primary goal being prevention of disease through the strengthening of the body's immune and musculoskeletal systems, and the regulation of respiratory and circulatory functions. It is not intended as a replacement for professional and timely medical care. The reader is urged to consult a medical professional on any matter concerning their health, and to follow the given diagnoses and prescriptions. Harking back to its classical, poetical roots, the Chinese language relies heavily on figures of speech such as hyperbole and metaphors, in order to evoke strong, multisensorial responses in the reader. While rendered in English translation some statements may seem definitive absolutes, they are rather meant to convey the rhetorical strength of a given argument in the original: they are to be taken for their suggestive, evocative power, rather than literally.

A CIP catalogue record for this title is available from the
British Library and the Library of Congress

ISBN 978 1 78775 520 8
eISBN 978 1 78775 521 5

Printed and bound in Great Britain by Clays Ltd.

Jessica Kingsley Publishers' policy is to use papers that are natural, renewable, and recyclable products and made from wood grown in sustainable forests. The logging and manufacturing processes are expected to conform to the environmental regulations of the country of origin.

Jessica Kingsley Publishers
73 Collier Street
London N1 9BE, UK

www.singingdragon.com

獻給所有追尋健康與智慧的你，願能受益於書中的竅訣及功法

澄

To all those seeking health and wisdom, may the knowledge and practices shared in this book benefit you on your path.

Wang Yun

EDITORS' PREFACE

Wang Yun's publications are varied and touch on many themes—from Daoism and health cultivation, to Buddhism, Confucianism, Chinese history, and even a novel. He is in the habit of producing these at a staggering rate of three to four volumes a year, and usually never consecutively writes two volumes in the same category, preferring to diversify his releases. We, however, have opted to stick to the same theme, and are pleased to offer here the second volume of Wang Yun's groundbreaking Daoist[1] trilogy.

The present offers both similarities with the first book, and its own particularities as well. The author continues to seamlessly infuse our minds with the concepts of the Daoist path of health and immortality, and its implications. He presents us with anecdotes from the lives of the founding fathers of his lineages, and in so doing conveys the spirit of the traditions they so passionately pursued and transmitted to posterity. Faced with the reality that many scholars lack practical experience, while many practitioners are missing a theoretical background, Wang Yun seeks here to bridge this gap, presenting us with both in equal measure.

Ever sensitive to the needs and particular circumstances of modern times, Wang Yun has done his utmost to simplify the sometimes arcane and complex practices handed down by generations of accomplished masters. Indeed, things have evolved in such a way that for all the commodities brought about by increased technological prowess, our lives seem busier and more occupied than ever before. With this concern in mind, Wang Yun has compiled and edited an astonishing amount of knowledge, to preserve and impart it on the one hand, but more

---

1 修道者 (xiudaozhe). A practitioner of either the philosophical, religious, or practical traditions of Daoism, which originated in China and emphasizes living in harmony with the Dao, or "the Way," the source, pattern, and substance of everything that exists, thereby becoming one with the unplanned rhythms of the universe. Also spelled Tao/Taoism/Taoist.

importantly—as he himself states—to provide us with the tools to cultivate the health and vitality so essential to a more comfortable, happy, and fulfilled life.

Above all, this text distinguishes itself from its counterparts in the trilogy by its practicality. Indeed, the text itself constitutes only the first, and smaller, part of the book: its bulk is a practice manual with detailed instructions and complementary pictures. This resource is invaluable to people nowadays—often lacking the time to pick out the instructions laced throughout the text— and testifies to Wang Yun's generosity, as he deplores in the text the narrow-minded covetousness, which led to the loss of many priceless lineages of practice. As we stated in our previous preface, the transmission of traditional teachings is essentially oral: not only that, it indeed demands a disciple demonstrate passion, discipline, fortitude, and above all trust and patience. Having amassed these teachings through decades of dedicated practice and service, Wang Yun is fond of recounting that the first instruction he received was to wash his teacher's cup—he sometimes had to scrub it clean up to a hundred times before his *sifu*[2] was satisfied. This is a lesson on patience, perseverance, and character: bereft of these, he would have never been able to walk the path he has. This, he maintains, is one of the most important teachings ever imparted to him.

Recollecting this story proved invigorating and inspiring, as we wrestled with such a nuanced and elegant text in a language foreign to us, one which at times required countless instances of translation, interpretation, editing, and rendering into plain, yet elegant, English.

In the first volume, *Climbing the Steps to Qingcheng Mountain*, the author takes us on a dance across time, through the history of China and Daoism, and through his memoirs of encounters with masters and fellow practitioners alike, with advice and practices sprinkled liberally throughout. While the somewhat elusive and free-spirited nature of Wang Yun's prose remains unaltered, in

---

2   師父 (*shifu*). A term of respect used to regard a master of some profession, especially where a lineage is involved. In terms of spelling, we have opted to defer to the popularized Cantonese form "sifu."

Part I of this volume, *daoyin*[3] is more focused in its purport. Two themes stand out as particularly salient: relaxation and the breath. In the matter of practices, the emphasis is clearly placed on posting, inasmuch as this foundational yet all-encompassing practice is an ideal tool to deepen one's experience of both relaxation and the breath. In Part II of this book, the reader will find a repository of exercises that wonderfully complement posting, such as the famed *Tendon Transformation Classic* of Bodhidharma—accessible tools to strengthen muscles, tendons, skeletal structure, and cultivate *qi*.[4]

All things between Heaven and Earth follow the ineluctable cycle of change, of rise and fall. So it was with our translation committee on the completion of *Climbing the Steps to Qingcheng Mountain*—seeing it come onto the market, and so well-received at that—our toil and sweat were rewarded with a book we could feel proud of, our gratification all the greater in the face of the enthusiasm that followed its publication. Yet, as with all things, the gust of elation was followed by the cooling breeze of another great truth of nature: a project completed is now a thing belonging to the past, and what lies ahead are the scores of treasures of wisdom Wang Yun so liberally conjures and shares with us.

The Modern Wisdom Translation Group team feels immensely indebted to the author for his selfless dedication to the well-being of others: we do hope you will feel likewise after practicing the exercises presented here. When asked how readers would benefit from reading his book, Wang Yun offered that its value lies in its practicality, that the reader will be able to ascertain proof of its content by the changes occurring in their own body with continued practice.

Not desirous to stand between the reader and their new spring, we now timely step aside and let you step into the precious, accessible marvels of *daoyin*.

Modern Wisdom Translation Group

---

3   導引 (*daoyin*). This was a precursor of *qigong*, and practiced by Daoists for health and spiritual cultivation.

4   氣 (*qi*). The vital force present in all living entities.

CONTENTS

PART 1: *DAOYIN*—AN OVERVIEW

PART 2: *DAOYIN*—TECHNIQUES

SECTION 1: POSTING FUNDAMENTALS

SECTION 2: BODHIDHARMA'S *YIJIN JING* (*TENDON TRANSFORMATION CLASSIC*)

SECTION 3: 養生九式 NINE STYLES FOR CULTIVATING HEALTH

SECTION 4: 奇經八脈簡易通脈功法 SIMPLIFIED EXERCISES TO OPEN UP THE EIGHT EXTRAORDINARY MERIDIANS

SECTION 5: CONCLUDING PRACTICES

DAOYIN— AN OVERVIEW

CHAPTER 1

POSTING AND *DAOYIN*

THE SKILL OF CLEANSING AND RESTORING

I met my Daoist *sifu* when I was around 17 or 18, and so began my training. First was the study of both meditation and posting, for *qi* cultivation. When there was time, *sifu* would talk about the origins of the practices and share anecdotes about the lineage and its masters. *Sifu* worried that I was too young in my understanding of the world and hoped the valuable words and precious spiritual knowledge passed down from immortal masters[1] of the past would cultivate both my outward decorum and inner temperament.

Now with my fiftieth year well behind me, I look back and liken my path of spiritual practice and internal cultivation to the metaphor of the "three beasts crossing the river":[2] the great generosity and kindness of my teachers was as high as a mountaintop, as long as a river. What they gave me is more than I could ever repay.

Of all the people *sifu* first told me about, two left the deepest impression: the first was Wang Zijin, a famous prince in the Warring States Period [the other was Peng Zu, whose story is in Chapter 3]. Wang Zijin met his Daoist master, Fu Qiugong, and followed him to Songshan[3] to practice austerities in order to

---

1   神仙人物 (*shenxianrenwu*). In Daoist terminology, the term "immortal" refers to an accomplished practitioner of Daoism. This immortality refers to the mindstate of one who lives content with time and abides in its passing. Their achievements are classified by their various degrees of extreme longevity. In the final stage, when the immortal "refines spirit into emptiness" (煉神化虛 *lianshenhuaxu*), the practitioner's physical body perishes, but the spirit permeates the entire universe.

2   三獸渡河 (*sanshouduhe*). Buddhist idiom: the metaphor of a rabbit, horse, and elephant crossing the river refers to three levels of accomplishment in the elimination of afflictions in Buddhism—namely Sravakayana, Pratyekabuddhayana, and Bodhisattvayana.

3   嵩山 (Songshan). In Henan province, China, the location of the famous Shaolin temple.

become a Daoist immortal. The Chinese poet Li Bai immortalized him in verse: "Do not follow the footsteps of Wang Zijin, who, having met Fuqiu, did all worldly matters forego." It is said that Wang Zijin had a penchant for music and fine literature, and was especially well versed in the reed pipe. When he played it, throngs of birds and other animals purportedly gathered to listen. Master Fu Qiugong admired Wang's cleverness, and so taught him the techniques of immortality. From that time on, Wang forgot about the affairs of the world.[4]

Forty years into his studies, Wang Zijin happened on an old acquaintance from his hometown. He implored him, saying, "Please tell my family that I hope to meet them on the seventh day of the seventh month of the lunar calendar..." On that given day, his family gathered at the designated meeting place. Suddenly, they all saw Wang riding a white crane through the mountains: with a smiling face he looked on them, and waved his hand as he gradually disappeared into the sky. His father Zhou Lingwang—the 11th Emperor of Eastern Zhou dynasty (571–545 BCE)—was late in receiving the news, and by the time he arrived his son had already "flown off."[5] Legend has it that, in order to leave a memento for him, Wang Zijin dropped from the sky the pair of cotton shoes that he had worn over his decades of Daoist practice. Many tales such as these surround the master and his enlightenment!

Sifu recounted that when he was learning *daoyin* and the posting stances, on Qingcheng Mountain,[6] his master gave him many tips regarding the techniques of internal cultivation. These all came from Wang Zijin, including the methods for breathing, exhaling, inhaling, and swallowing *qi*. They included also the one that *sifu* often reminded us of: to completely relax the body

---

4   忘了世俗之事 (*wangleshisuzhishi*). In Daoism and Buddhism, the concept of "forgetting about worldly affairs" refers to the single-mindedness of the true practitioner who undertakes the spiritual path with such focus as to become completely unconcerned with the mundane, ordinary affairs of the world. This does not mean they ignore or neglect their duties in the world: simply, they are not concerned, moved, or affected by them.

5   駕鶴登天 (*jiahedengtian*). In Daoist lore, to "fly up into the sky" was a common way to describe the passing of a great master.

6   青城山 (Qingchengshan). In Sichuan province, China.

before meditating—after loosening up, you must stretch the hands forward, then lower the palms and slowly breathe from the nose. Another technique begins the same way: after relaxing the body and inhaling through the nose, you hold the breath and shake the head right, left, and all around dozens of times. Then there's the method for full relaxation of the body that involves lying flat on a bed,[7] slowly exhaling the impure *qi*.[8] This is followed by inhaling through the nose deeply, slowly breathing into the area between the chest and stomach, and swallowing and holding the *qi*. In brief, when it comes to refining the *qi*, to the practice of *daoyin*, to inhalation and exhalation, one ought to apply to meditation and *qi* cultivation all the nearly 100 other oral tips[9] passed down by the immortal Wang Zijin. If you experience any obstruction regarding *qi*, muscles or internal organs, you can use these very methods to cleanse and restore the body.

---

7   沒有寒氣的床 (*meiyoudongqidechuang*). Traditional Chinese medicine mentions that the bed should be devoid of "cold *qi*," the idea being that the "coldness" of the bed is absorbed by the body and may cause illness. Decades ago, when the instructions were given, beds in Taiwan were not as warm and cozy as they are now, and getting ill from this was rather common.

8   濁氣 (*zhuoqi*). Some *qigong* practices involve exhaling the "foul" or "impure" *qi* of the body: any impurities or unhealthy *qi* that exist and stagnate in the body, causing discomfort and illness.

9   口訣 (*koujue*). A special instruction given by the teacher to help develop a student's practice. 竅訣 (*qiaojue*), a "pertinent clue" given to practitioners at the right time to improve their practice, is also of similar meaning.

CHAPTER 2

SIFU'S HEARTFELT LEGACY

Throughout his lifelong quest to "return to the truth" and reach the heights of the path of the immortals, *sifu's* reverence of a select few Daoist predecessors helped drive him along relentlessly until he passed away. His admiration extended even further, to the many practitioners in history who diligently followed the same path: Laozi, and a succession of those who cultivated the inner pill[1] and practiced cultivation exercises—Guang Chengzi, Ge Hong, Wei Boyang, Zhong Liquan, Lu Chunyang, Qiu Changchun among them. Incidentally, during his stay on Hua Mountain[2] in his early years, *sifu* encountered by chance a Daoist master who taught him the immortal Ge Hong's *Qimen Dunjia* divination practice. In the early stages of my own practice, he then exhorted me to read the *Misty Fisherman Song*.[3]

The explanations on the origin of *Qimen Dunjia* to date are varied, and I have also heard several elder Daoist masters speak on the subject. Its early history is not unlike a novel or a movie, such as those about Zhu Geliang, the talented military strategist, or Chi You, the mythical founder of metalworking. It's very likely that history and mythology both play a part in this tale. Historically, Chi You is described as a giant, like the tallest NBA (National Basketball Association) players of our time. He was born as sturdy as a fortress, impervious to the strikes of a blade, and

---

1 丹道養生家 (*dandaoyangshengjia*). The inner pill refers to the alchemical process undergone in the practice of *daoyin* where essence is transformed into *qi*, which is transformed into spirit.

2 華山 (Huashan). In Shaanxi province, one of the five great mountains of China, with a long history of religious significance.

3 煙波釣叟歌 (*yanbodiaosouge*). A poetry-based commentary of *Qimen Dunjia*, outlining its principles. By fully comprehending it, one is said to be holding the key to the system.

could summon the forces of the elements. If at that time the Yellow Emperor, Huang Di, hadn't used the *Qimen Dunjia* transmitted by "the dark lady of the nine heavens,"[4] then perhaps his critical battle against Chi You would have been lost, impacting the ending of the Han dynasty and the beginning of the Ming and possibly steering history on an entirely different course! Consequently, this miraculous version of the *Qimen Dunjia* served as the foundation for the divination schools of the *Daliuren, Taiyishenshu,*[5] and *Qimen Dunjia.*

Since its inception, the *Qimen Dunjia* divination method has gone through over a thousand modifications before settling on the modern simplified version with its nine configurations. This modification process started with the Daoist hermit Huang Shigong and his successors before the final changes by the strategist Zhang Liang (3rd century–186 BCE) brought the modern practice into its current form, known as the "Nine States of the *Yindun* and *Yangdun.*"

When I was young, *sifu* thought my foundations not solid enough to begin studying the *Book of Changes,*[6] so instead he lent me a copy of the *Imperial Encyclopedia,*[7] compiled by the elder Song He; this included parts about divination, for my reference. I undertook the mind-numbing mission of spending whole days committing all of the verses within to memory, an unforgettable experience to say the least. *Sifu* himself had made significant contributions to the "purple star astrology"[8] divination method: in those days, no one in Taiwan had even heard of it, and most

---

4 九天玄女 (*Jiutianxuannu*). A significant goddess in Daoism, teacher to the Yellow Emperor. She brought him *feng shui*, among many other things, allowing him to win a famous battle against Chi You. Also translated as "the mysterious lady of the ninth heaven."

5 大六壬, 太乙神數. Along with *Qimen Dunjia*, these are two of the three major forms of divination originating in China.

6 易經 (*Yi Jing*). Ancient Chinese divination text, the oldest Chinese classic. Also known in the west as *I-Ching*.

7 古今圖書 (*Gujintushu*). Ten-thousand-scroll encyclopedia of premodern China, compiled around 1701–1706.

8 紫微斗數 (*ziweidoushu*). Popular form of divination in Chinese culture, used to determine an individual's destiny.

practiced either the methods of "four pillars of destiny astrology,"[9] or types of face and palm reading that had been passed down from their ancestors. At a young age, *sifu* had encountered a rather talented man who passed on to him the *purple star* method: he could thus look at the palm of the hand and, in less than three minutes and without asking any questions, clearly determine the time and date of a person's birth, the house of their zodiac sign, and their astrological affinity.[10] I later used this method to predict movements in the stock market! This was the era before computers: the system required only a birth year, month, day, and time, coupled with a photo, and a complete astrological chart would thus emerge.

Sifu mentioned to me that the modern-day *purple star* astrology is incomplete. He selflessly instructed: "Ultimately, in the four planets of the tenth heavenly stem, *Pojun* stands for fortune, *Jumen* is authority, *Taiyin* is knowledge, and *Tanlang* is fear.[11] The current system stops there." He continued: "After this, there is actually a whole lot more." Furthermore, *sifu's* method of *purple star* divination was unrelated to Chen Tuan[12]—the hermit ancestor from Huashan—and his sect. Why was this the case? In order to make it absolutely clear and understandable. As these ancient practices move into modern times, I contemplate how to keep the wheel turning, how to pass the secrets on...how to share the depth of my knowledge in the years to come.

In order to teach me how to accurately understand face reading, and the finest details of people's complexion, *sifu* instructed me to sit in a dark room with threads of the five colors [five colors particular to the Complete Reality school of the Daoist tradition],

---

9   子平八字 (*zipingbazi*). Currently one of the more popular forms of divination: details about a person's time of birth are used to determine their fate. Also called "eight characters."

10   甲乙丙級星宿到四化 (*jiayibingjixingxiudaosihua*). Like Western astrology, Chinese astrology divides people among the 12 signs of the zodiac, and then ever more finely by star. The meaning of the passage is that *sifu* could determine many fine layers of complexity at first sight.

11   破軍,巨門,太陰,貪狼 (*Pojun, Jumen, Taiyin, Tanlang*). Four significant planets in the *purple star* astrology system.

12   陳摶 (Chen Tuan). 907–960 CE, famed Daoist sage, creator of the sleeping *qigong* and one of *sifu's* lineage masters.

and look at them intently, practicing until I may be able to discern an individual's complexion at a glance, as though they were transparent. I thus developed the ability to read a face and determine someone's zodiac and luck. Over the course of the next ten years or so, following my interest and curiosity, I delved into the study of *yin* and *yang* theory, perceiving their essence, and consulting *sifu* when any difficulty arose. Little by little, without fail, I made many fruitful achievements, and successfully developed my practice. I obtained a complete and perfect understanding of the theory, acquired skill in geomancy, and made numerous breakthroughs. I often reminisce about these experiences. I'm filled with immense gratitude and absolute wonder at being on the receiving end of *sifu's* wide-ranging and profound wisdom. It is this that supported me in the early days, and helped me find strength on the path to increasing and fulfilling my karmic connections.

CHAPTER 3

AS ANCIENT AS PENG ZU

DAOYIN SECRETS TO HEALTH

Sifu always used to tell me that Daoism is China's native religion, and its culture the offspring of the Hundred Schools of Thought.[1] From the Yellow Emperor to Laozi, from Zhuangzi to Liezi, Shang Yang and the *Han Feizi* that later formed the Legalist School,[2] Huang Shigong, Sunzi ("Sun Tzu"), and the *Guiguzi*[3] that formed the Military School, Jiang Ziya and Zhang Liang,[4] known for their military strategy: all of these renowned figures of lore emerged within the context of these philosophical and religious traditions. If you studied the central tenets and philosophies of any one of these schools, you would find that none strayed far from the sagacious and illustrious figures that upheld the Daoist path. This is the character and bloodline that sets Chinese culture apart from all others: as the descendants of *Yanhuang*, we have a duty to preserve our ancient wisdom.

With regards to *daoyin*, aside from the cultivation practices of the Daoist master Wang Zijin, *sifu* would also frequently touch on the essential instructions left by Peng Zu. Peng Zu is commonly known in legend and lore as a man who lived to be 800 years old. Yet another version of his legend according to the Wudang and Qingcheng schools was told to me by a Daoist elder, clarifying that

---

1 諸子百家 (*zhuzibaijia*). The varying schools of thought and their exponents during the Spring and Autumn and Warring States periods.

2 法家一系 (*Fajiayixi*). Philosophical school from the Warring States period (475–221 BCE), formed the ideological basis of the Qin dynasty (221–207 BCE).

3 鬼谷子 (*Guiguzi*). A group of writings compiled between the late Warring States period and the end of the Han dynasty, discussing techniques of political lobbying based in Daoist thinking.

4 張良 (Zhang Liang). Famous fugitive-turned-strategist, and advisor to generals and leaders during the establishment of the Han dynasty.

the 800 years of Peng Zu's life is not a figure to be taken literally but a number based on an ancient sexegenary cycle used for calculating a person's age.

One year in our current, 365-days system is equal to only two months in the ancient sexegenary one; this would put Peng Zu's "real age" at just over 130 years. Different theories exist, placing his age at anywhere from 840 to 880 sexegenary years, which would put his life span at just beyond 150 years!

Pinpointing the exact dates for Peng Zu's life and death is ultimately beside the point—he nonetheless distinguished himself by his very advanced age, a peak that few throughout history ever reached. Among these were the distinguished Chinese medicine doctor Sun Simiao, who maintained a life of virtue and upright conduct. His attention from day to day was focused solely on inner cultivation and Daoist breathing techniques. His diet and sleep were strictly regulated. Things of the world like fame, reputation, and personal gain, he saw as wisps of cloud. All of these elements combined to carry him past 140 years. Another was Zhang Sanfeng, founder and abbot of the first monastery of the Wudang Sect;[5] he is said to have lived to over 200 years. Another, Master Li Qingyun, lived to see the early years of the Republic of China, ascending to over 250 years of age before his passing. Not only that, but he racked up over 20 marriages and close to 200 offspring! He once let slip some of the secrets to his abnormally long life, including following a vegetarian diet, and a life-long avoidance of eggs and milk. The other was his detachment from the emotions and desires that normally rule your life—he always kept his mind still like a pool of undisturbed water. Then there was his understanding and application of medicine and pharmacology, and especially his authority in Chinese herbal prescriptions. According to records, he was given national honors, after turning a century old, for his outstanding contributions to Chinese medicine.

Coming back to Peng Zu, perhaps now he is seen as a somewhat eccentric and otherworldly figure, but his name has been traditionally

---

5 武當派 (*wudangpai*). Wudang school. Although sometimes cited as a fictional sect in martial arts novels, this sect originated in the Wudang mountains. It was founded in the early Yuan dynasty by Zhang Sanfeng, a renowned Daoist immortal.

respected and revered throughout the generations of Chinese culture. Some of China's great sages, like Confucius and Zhuangzi, spoke of his name and ideas. He was even recorded in Ge Hong's[6] *Biographies of the Deities and Immortals*, and Zhuangzi's *Free and Easy Wandering*. All of this merely illustrates the revered position he was held in as an immortal. Zhuangzi employs various metaphors in his essay, speaking of turtles, trees, cicadas, and fungi to convey a sense of urgency and uncertainty about the length of time we have in this world but in the end is unable to avoid mentioning the man who seemed to defy aging. Peng Zu's almost unsurpassable durability is seen as linked to his diet, his cultivation practices, and *qigong*, earning him the right to be compared with proverbial symbols of longevity such as the turtle and crane.

---

6   葛洪 (Ge Hong). A Jin dynasty Daoist practitioner and alchemist (283–363 CE).

CHAPTER 4

THE ESSENTIALS OF COMPLETE, UTTER RELAXATION

While the immortal Peng Zu lived among us, he handed down to later generations the practices for maintaining health, as well as the longevity techniques he had acquired. With my Daoist *sifu*, I studied nearly 20 forms of *daoyin*, as well as a few breathing techniques: these were extremely effective during meditation, and in treating blockages of the channels.

At a young age, *sifu* was living in the mountains, and at one point had to travel to a remote place to collect firewood. It was the rainy season, the paths rugged and slippery from precipitation. He lost his footing and fell into a ravine, bruising both his abdomen and rib cage. Although he used *tuina*[1] from the Daoist tradition, and bone-setting techniques to treat his injuries for close to a year, whenever the season changed, he experienced pain and blood clotting in the injured areas. He would suffer incredible pain from this, until Master Jing Tai transmitted to him an ancient breathing practice passed down by the Daoist master Chi Songzi. This brought about his rapid recovery, and ten doses of Chinese herbal medicine were enough to remove the stagnation and get him off medication entirely. From that point on, he practiced daily, with great persistence, according to the special oral tip described by the immortal Chi Songzi, which begins: "breathe out the old, dirty *qi*, breathe in the new, pure *qi*…"

Sifu told me once that almost all schools of Daoism describe Chi Songzi as an ancient rain god. To this day, there are temples in many areas dedicated to him. *Sifu* also heard that this rain god

---

1　推拿 (*tuina*). A form of Chinese massage therapy often used in conjunction with other practices to treat musculoskeletal pain and disability.

hailed from the time of Shen Nong (the god of farming):[2] all the food, water, and jade that Shen Nong took was passed on to him from Chi Songzi himself!

From the time he was young, *sifu* had come across different traditional versions of Chi Songzi's anecdotes. He added that regardless of tradition, he would follow the oral tips and techniques passed down from these old generations. To this day, he has been able to maintain good health, fortune, and longevity through these very practices, without the need to question or investigate these traditional stories and folklore.

These ancient methods are extremely simple when used in practice; they are not like those developed by people in modern times, loaded with trivial and complicated details. Many times, *sifu* would show me how he practiced, how he coordinated his movement with the breath. There are 18 different movements altogether: he said most of the *qigong* used to cure physical ailments, which has been popular to this day, actually originates from the methods mentioned above, passed down by successive generations of practitioners. He continued by saying that, of course, were he to truly expound on these methods, there would be too much to discuss. Indeed, were I to explain it in detail—expounding on traditional *daoyin* exercises, breathing methods, and practices—I'm afraid it would take up an unreasonable amount of time, and this wouldn't be the right approach to the introduction of these methods.

The *Neijing*[3] advocates for "a quiet demeanour that doesn't yield to fame or gain, from which the pure *qi* can arise; a composed spirit that wards off all potential diseases." From the viewpoint of Traditional Chinese Medicine (TCM), this passage already contains the most important distinction on breathing. The breath of someone who is often in poor physical condition is relatively short and unsettled, coarse and unstable. Unbeknown to them, this is already an indication of illness present in that individual's internal organs. However, someone whose physical energy is

---

2   神農. This deity dates back to 2000 BCE and is credited with the invention of agriculture.

3   黃帝內經 (*Huangdi Neijing*). An ancient Chinese medical text regarded as the fundamental doctrinal source for Chinese medicine for more than two millennia. Composed of two texts, each of 81 chapters.

maintained at a high and healthy state will appear peaceful and at ease at all times.

The way *qigong* is currently practiced stresses the importance of maintaining focus on a specific place—the aim being to "hold" an acupuncture point. This will allow the distracted mind to become focused, and is referred to as "guarding the acupoints." Through the focus on adjusting the breath, breathing will become consistent, deep, long, and fine, as precisely as a gossamer thread goes through a needle. In this way, you won't even hear your own breath, and you can use this method of breathing in both moving and still practices. Breathing this way will awaken the potential of the brain, mind, and lungs. It also assists the movement of *qi* through the twelve and eight extraordinary channels,[4] which will have a positive effect on the internal organs. In the past, when I was practicing *qigong* and *daoyin*, I benefited greatly from what my teacher passed on to me. He taught me how to be deeply relaxed; how to let things move easily; how to unite the mind and its thoughts and not be disturbed by external or internal circumstances; how to focus the mind and not set limits on the idea of "fullness" or "emptiness"; how to mix *yin* and *yang*. Only by applying all of this will you begin to appreciate the profoundness of these exercises.

I have always had the habit of collecting stories from fellow practitioners and sharing them with others. Over the course of many years, I've been able to confirm my own experiences through these exchanges. Although it took a very long time—for a while I put all of my energy into the study of Buddhist classics and the contemplation of *Chan* verses—this period of time was more valuable than gold. Though I was not as energetic in the study of the path of immortals as my teacher was, on reflection I could no longer keep these precious teachings hidden, so I decided to share them. Furthermore, as some of my students have been asking me to teach on these matters for the past few decades, despite the meager amount I had obtained from my studies, I've decided to select a few simple cultivation exercises as an introduction of sorts, to share with those who are destined to find a connection.

---

4   十二經絡,奇經八脈 (*shierjingluo, qijingbamai*). Some of the pathways through which *qi* circulates through the body.

CHAPTER 5

MEDITATION AND *DAOYIN*

MOTIVATION AND PERSEVERANCE

When learning *qigong* and *daoyin*, it's important not to be in a rush to see results, and to understand that all of the body's ailments have their underlying causes. Some of these conditions may be attributed to long-term negligence from a young age; some may be from recklessly bringing injury on the body and swindling away health and energy with abandon. In these cases, it's usually only when medicine is no longer of any use and the doctors have nothing left to try, that people will turn to *qigong* and *daoyin* in order to save their health. Some people wait until they're given the final countdown and sent home to live out their last days, then they come waving and shouting with their last-ditch plea to be thrown the *qigong* liferaft. Others study in order to master the ancient arts of the immortals and gain supernatural abilities. In summary, each person has their own set of reasons and causes that brings them into contact with meditation and *qigong*.

According to my personal experience, if the problems you are experiencing are rooted in karma or caused by those beings to whom you may be karmically indebted,[1] then you must resort to purification practices, the accumulation of merit through good works, and your own private efforts to effect internal change. Through such means of cleansing the spirit, in combination with meditation and *qi* exercises, in some cases it is possible to make a full recovery without medicine. All in all, approach your practice with steadfast composure and tireless zeal but without yearning

---

1   This school of Daoism values the concept of "karma," or cause and effect looked at over the span of several lifetimes, and taken as the root cause for conditions in this life. "Karmic debt" implies a cause for which there has not yet been an effect, leaving a karmic debt, which will have to be repaid at a future time.

for more, without craving instant and spectacular results. Practice in this way, and like mountain rain that one day gathers and forms a river, your achievements will build and grow strong. These are words that I hope will bring strength and encouragement to all those with a connection.

Meditation and daoyin *are not miraculous panaceas just sitting in an unlocked treasure chest; their potency requires people of a resolute will and perseverance to discover them.* We don't live in the world of novels, TV dramas, or legends where the governing and conception channels[2] and the rest of the eight extraordinary channels are opened as easily as your front door. In today's world, so completely pervaded by notions of utilitarianism, it is a wonderful thing indeed if people can simply persist in daily meditation and *qigong*. In the process, they are doing themselves an incredible favor.

The term *qigong* itself is actually modern. In the records of the immortals in ancient China, the term *daoyin* was used to convey the extension of life by means of exercises involving movement and breathing that cultivate the body's *qi*. The most oft-quoted text is a passage from the *Records of the Three Kingdoms*, which makes special mention of things relating to *daoyin*: "Imitate the action of the bear climbing a tree trunk and the owl looking behind, pulling the waist and the body, letting all the joints move in order to slow down aging." In this text "bear" and "owl" movements refer to practices that originated from ancient *qi* practitioners and Daoist alchemists who practiced in mountain forests, observing and mimicking the movements of flying birds and walking animals. After witnessing and experiencing the wondrous effects of such movements, these practitioners of lore entered them into the volume of exercises that exist to this day.

The bear movements stem from observations such as these: when a large bear is lazily foraging for food near a tree, it will hug the trunk and shimmy itself up with a movement similar to the way

---

2   任督二脈 (*renduermai*). Two energy channels in the body that play a primary role in *qigong* practice and together form the microcosmic orbit. The *Ren* channel runs through the center of the front, ventral, portion of the body. The *Du* channel runs through the center of the back, dorsal, portion of the body.

gymnasts pull themselves up on parallel bars. The only difference is that the feet do not leave the ground. There's also the "looking owl," which is mentioned in the *Shijing Guofeng*.[3] Owls can be regarded as comparatively aggressive birds: some say this family of birds, also known as the "cat's head hawk," has its origins in the rainforest. When tired from hunting prey, an owl can often be spotted sitting still in a tree, twisting its head while keeping the rest of its body motionless—it regains its energy this way. It's said that owls also have the distinctive ability to turn their heads through a 270° range, which surpasses human limitations. If someone in this day and age has not learned or regularly practiced this movement, and repeatedly twists their head like an owl, they would actually put great strain on their arteries, to the point of risking a stroke. Ancient practitioners observed the swivel of the owl's head and incorporated it into their *daoyin* exercises to circulate the *qi* and blood and preserve their health.

Whether it's the tiger, deer, ape, bear, or bird movements, all the styles of the "five animal exercises" given to future generations of practitioners mimic the natural behavior of animals in mountains and forests. It is believed that copying these movements with the body is a way to dispel illness, moving the limbs and bones while stretching and opening all of the joints.

From later generations of practitioners who sought truth and achieved the elixir of immortality came a steady contribution to the volume of *daoyin* exercises, based on their observations of nature's cycles and animals. Take Zhong Liquan (also known as Han Zhongli), one of the Eight Immortals and the founder of the School of Complete Reality (*Quanzhen*) during the Eastern Han dynasty (25–220 CE). Originally, he was a general who led troops on the battlefield; after a particular defeat, he wandered dejectedly into the Zhongnan mountains[4] and there encountered the spirit of Emperor Dong Hua. In the historical records of Daoist deities, Dong Hua was always the one who, together with Xi Wangmu

---

3   詩經國風. The first part of the Classic of Poetry, one of the "Five Classics" of Chinese literature, said to have been compiled by Confucius, and the oldest known collection of Chinese poetry.

4   終南山. A mountain range near Xi'an, in Shanxi province, China.

(the "Western Queen Mother"), presided over male and female spirits in Heaven: anyone who wished for a place in the heavens of the immortals had to go through him. As such, he occupies a peculiarly elevated position within the *Quanzhen* school. Dong Hua transmitted the essential instructions on attaining immortality to Zhong Liquan who, after enduring his training on Yangjiao Mountain, eventually achieved immortality. Later on, he also came across Iron-crutch Li,[5] who taught him the alchemy for turning stone into gold; this ability enabled Zhong Liquan to go on and help those in suffering, accumulating great merit (good karma). Even later on, he attained complete achievement.[6]

Successive generations within the School of Complete Reality all possess a memorial tablet paying tribute to its founder, Zhong Liquan.

---

5   李鐵拐 (Li Tieguai). One of the Eight Immortals in Chinese mythology. He walked around with an iron crutch and carried a gourd with special medicine.

6   Daoist achievement generally refers to specific levels of immortality or admittance into certain levels of the Daoist heaven or even directly ascending into heaven while alive.

CHAPTER 6

Intertwined Mind and Breath

I should take a moment to mention an important instruction *sifu* gave me early on in my studies: he urged me to spend time contemplating and constantly reinforcing my practice with his selected picks of the recorded sayings of the old patriarchs. Whether in the study of meditation, internal alchemy, or the cultivation of health through *qigong* and *daoyin*, he said these teachings would be of decidedly great benefit on the path of practice.

This collection of recorded sayings was presented as a gift by *sifu's* master during the year he spent "seeking the Dao" on Qingcheng Mountain. The passages within are majestic and profound, without being gilded or abstruse, and I read through them with great joy. Along the same lines, the guidance they contain on inner cultivation and spiritual practice is wonderfully transformative for the body and soul. *Sifu* would always say that thinking back to his time on the mountain, he felt deeply blessed to have returned with so many treasures. *Sifu* would often mention that cultivating *qi* is not something accomplished merely through the physical form of the exercise. In whatever practice you undertake, the mind and breath must be united. This can be done through the physical form or the methods of breathing. At a deeper level, the body and soul must be united. Cultivating *qi*, as opposed to simple physical exercise is key.

These are the unique aspects of *sifu's* teaching style that I experienced during my training at his residence.

Sifu required that my training begin from the physical exercises. I progressed through each form of posting, holding a single posture for a minimum of three hours and wrapping up each session with the *qi pian quan shen*[1] closing exercise. My clothes would regularly cycle between dry and sweat-drenched. All of this exertion aimed to remove any obstructions to the free circulation of *qi* through the eight extraordinary channels and twelve organ channels, and to prevent *qi* from stagnating at any of the acupoints, or anywhere else along the energy channels. For this training to work, you must not let temper get in the way: even a single angry thought would waylay your best efforts. There was definitely a logic behind this aspect of *sifu's* instructions.

You may notice that certain people have discolorations or scars that look like sunspots (also known as liver spots) covering their face. How are these formed? As soon as our anger rises, all of the *qi* and blood in the body will rush to the head. Not only does this rapidly deplete oxygen in the blood, but it also creates toxins that interact with the skin and hair follicles, resulting in inflammation and other skin-related problems, including the formation of sunspots on the face.

The sympathetic nervous system of people who regularly lose their temper is strained and overstimulated. Most likely this means their heart isn't getting sufficient oxygen and their liver function has been impaired or damaged. When in the sway of rage, regardless of whether it is released or suppressed, your body secretes catecholamines—stress hormones that cause both a rapid spike in blood sugar levels and the speeding up of fat breakdown. In turn, there is a sizable increase in the concentration of toxins in the liver cells. This kind of information is now readily available thanks to the recent emergence of detailed medical research reports and clinical studies on this subject; the lineage masters of the past warned us of these dangers long before modern medical research arrived. This is a keen reminder not to overlook the critical impact emotions and the breath have on our health.

Whatever upsetting events might have occurred on the previous day, I always advise practitioners to get up early and coax a smile out of themselves to begin their day. Face yourself in the mirror

---

1 氣遍全身 (*qipianquanshen*). A *qigong* practice from the category of "concluding exercises," meant to balance and circulate the *qi* throughout the body at the end of a practice session.

and give yourself a big, wide grin, repeating this 21 times: as long as you smile, all the cells in your body will set your feet on a healthy path. If you're really caught in the thick of your emotions, you can recite the *Heart Sutra*[2] to settle the waves. A special technique beginners can employ is to recite one word at a time, keeping your eyes and mind undividedly focused on each individual word. Once your body and mind have relaxed and you finish reciting three rounds of the sutra, you will have already transformed your anger. And when you've reached the point where you've memorized all the words, you will be able to recite it as quickly as if you were reciting a mantra, and can finish a full round in a single breath. To "match the breath with the recitation," do as follows: first take a deep breath, and after the *qi* enters the *dantian*,[3] recite the sutra from memory, stopping only when you run out or breath. Then pause, take another full inhalation, and finish reciting the sutra.

In the process of recitation, your mind and spirit must be in unison with the text—you cannot become distracted. Once you have recited a certain number of times, your negative emotions will have dispersed like a mist. If you wish to amplify the power of the blessings[4] when reciting the *Heart Sutra*, you can visualize Guanyin[5] in the space in front of you. Guanyin's figure is white as snow and translucent like crystal, radiating light on to your body. When distracting thoughts enter the mind, recite the sutra while visualizing Guanyin, and you might find some pretty incredible results!

In brief, there are countless ways to recite the *Heart Sutra*, the aforementioned just being a few examples. In times when your mind is all over the place, or when your anger is uncontrollable, I entreat you to use these techniques to placate it and find respite.

---

2 般若波羅蜜多心經 (*Banruoboluomiduo Xinjing*). The *Heart of Prajna Paramita Sutra* or *Heart Sutra* is one of the most popular sutras from a collection of about 40 Mahayana Buddhist texts of varying lengths known as the *Prajnaparamita Sutras*.

3 丹田 (*dantian*). Literally means "red field" or "cinnabar field." It is a focal point for most *qigong* and meditation practices, located approximately four finger-widths below the navel, inside the lower abdomen.

4 加持 (*jiachi*). In Buddhist terms, "blessings" can refer to any kind of benefit derived from a practice, from the mundane to the more subtle and esoteric.

5 觀世音菩薩 (*Guanshiyin Pusa*). Also known as Avalokiteśvara, the Buddhist bodhisattva of compassion, featured in the *Heart Sutra*, and also recognized in Daoist schools. Represented in either female and male form in different times and traditions.

CHAPTER 7

REST YOUR MIND

STILL AND UNATTACHED

As detailed in the *Seven Sages of the School of Complete Reality*, Ma Danyang's[1] conduct throughout life was irreproachable. Most importantly, the insights he provided based on his lifelong practice of Daoism have immensely benefited later generations. While some might find his writings absurd and difficult to the point of wanting to skip over them, or give up altogether, do not pass by the gems hidden within! The patriarch warned his readers repeatedly of the toxic effects of alcohol, and was often quoted saying, "If a practitioner drinks alcohol, the course of their channels will fall into disarray; if he indulges himself in a lady's chamber, his spiritual practice will be haunted."

The patriarch adopted an "at ease" approach in his daily affairs: please do not overlook the importance of being "at ease!" For a Daoist practitioner, the meaning of "at ease" surpasses even the poetry illustrated in these verses:

> *At ease and I see osmanthus flowers falling*
> *A night so still, a mountain so hollow in spring.*
> *Up comes the moon awaking the mountain birds,*
> *By the brook in spring, then and again they sing.*[2]

---

1   馬丹陽. Disciple of the immortal Wang Chongyang, himself the disciple of Zhong Liquan (the founder of the School of Complete Reality). Ma Danyang began the lineage that Wang Yun is now the holder and perpetuator of. See Chapter 10 for more details.

2   Excerpt from "Birdsong Brook," by Wang Wei (701–761). Translated by Andrew W.F. Wong. Wang Wei and the poet Du Fu were contemporaries and are generally considered, along with Li Bai, as representing the Buddhist, Daoist, and Confucian strands of Chinese culture.

A practitioner's mind is settled, in a constant state of stillness while in the midst of all external phenomena, because there is nothing in it to cause concern. Their mind is like an unspoilt pool of clear water that is without source or substance, unbound in the expanse of Heaven and Earth. The vastness and quietude of such "ease" is drastically different from the feigned ease and confidence of a lamenting, dejected poet.

Inordinately proud of his talents yet despairing over his lack of recognition, Du Fu[3] passed himself off as a free and merry spirit frolicking through the mountain springs and forests, unrestrained by mundane affairs. However, an astute reader can spot the grudges he held and the suffering and pain he inflicted on himself from the mental shackles he could not escape.

Take this poem:

> *We go against the white waves, churning on,*
> *a clear view spreads before me far and wide.*
> *Luckily the boat moves slowly*
> *and I can see all the fine wonders we are passing through.*
> *Kongling, height of rose-cloud rock,*
> *maple and juniper hide precipitous steeps.*
> *Green spring still acts without favorite,*
> *but the bright sun shines here especially.*
> *I could have my dwelling built here*
> *once and for all entrust my long whistling here.*
> *Poisonous miasmas are not worth worrying about,*
> *but men in arms fill the frontier regions.*
> *From before a lingering regret remains,*
> *I am shamed by the mockery of men of full understanding.*
> *I hope to prolong my appreciation when I sail back,*
> *but of this fine place, I comprehend the essentials.*[4]

Doesn't this poem truthfully portray Du's state of mind? An ordinary person carelessly weaves their life out of the desires and schemes each day brings, akin to a tiny boat thrown about by the

---

3 杜甫. A prominent poet of the Tang dynasty.
4 Excerpt from *The Poetry of Du Fu*, translated and edited by Stephen Owen. Published by Walter de Gruyter, GmbH & Co KG.

ocean waves. Though all beings are born equal, if you look around at the lives of others, you would see how every single person is helplessly tugged along by the strings of their destiny. Some live like lonely stones scattered across the edge of a cliff, wearing away each day on the precipice of oblivion without a soul to care for them. Even if they drift away in a makeshift raft or seek the comfortable solitude of their shell, in the end they may not escape the crafty claws of fate.

It is a mistake to view someone who flees to the forest to escape the challenges and distressing conditions of the world as gracefully free. If a person fails to see through the true nature of all affairs, it will be too late for them to feel regret when they enter the bardo.[5] Therefore, Ma Danyang would often remind his disciples to never get too attached, even when everything is going splendidly. Is this not an echo of what the Buddhist masters teach when they say, "Hurry past the Buddha when he is there; never dwell where he is not?" I also encourage my students with the following stanza, "At ease and yet always crystal clear; nothing left to do yet always in stillness." If a practitioner has already reached the point where nothing from this world "sticks" in their mind (having an adverse effect on its balance), that is true *at ease*. If they are buried in the reading of the classics and other texts but can comprehend the underlying meaning behind the words, then they are fully settled within any and all circumstances.

That said, can you really comprehend lineage master Ma Danyang's underlying meaning of "a practitioner free and at ease?" If a practitioner cannot perceive the dual emptiness of both subject and object, and haven't the skill to unlock the inner, outer, and lower *dantian*, what hope would they ever have of returning to the primordial state of "neither arising nor cessation?" Once you complete the requisite training to the level of "turtle breathing,"[6]

---

5   中陰 (*zhongyin*). In general, any state of transition, here referring specifically to the transitional state between death and rebirth, according to Buddhist tradition.

6   鶴胎龜息 (*hetaiguixi*). In "turtle breathing" one must make the mind return to the state it experienced while in the mother's womb, free from any desire and complicated thoughts. Nor is there any breathing through the mouth or nose—all the *qi* enters through the navel. This is in fact the fundamental principle.

you would ascend naturally to a state of "purity and non-action."[7] In the recorded sayings of Ma Danyang, he warned that *qi* is the most difficult thing to harness, akin to trying to ride a wild horse. It is difficult for the mind to quiet down because it is prone to chase after everything your eyes perceive, making it hard to loosen your grip on fame and fortune. He further emphasized that practitioners must persist in keeping their mind as if it were stowed away deep in a mountain valley: every thought comes from "no mind." The crux here is this "no mind"—to enter stillness through practicing *qi*, it is paramount to base meditation and *qigong* practices on "no-thing."

What is "no-thing"? Novice practitioners are undoubtedly baffled by the idea of "no-thingness." Before they are able to master the higher level practices, they ought to start working with the outer version of nothingness by utilizing the intention. When starting meditation, *daoyin*, *qigong*, or posting, first visualize that every part of your body—starting from the hair and all the way down to the chest, back, lower back, legs, and finally to the *yongquan*[8] points on the soles of your feet—becomes empty. Repeatedly suggest to yourself: "all of my hair, skin, and bones are intrinsically empty." Gradually, you will experience emptiness. The key and basis for practicing *qigong* and *daoyin* is that the mind should not cling to any objects. If it does, it immediately becomes distracted and falls prey to the various sensations of soreness, itchiness, swollenness, pain, numbness, and the urge to move around. When the mind is distracted by these fine sensations, true *qi* cannot rise. If true *qi* cannot rise, all efforts are for naught. Before I teach any exercises, I want you to bear in mind these relevant points that I drew from the *Recorded Sayings of Patriarch Ma Danyang*.

---

7   清靜無為 (*qingjingwuwei*). Non-action is an important concept in Daoism, being both an attitude, motivated by a lack of desire to participate in human affairs, and a technique by which someone may gain an enhanced control of human affairs.

8   湧泉 (*yongquan*). An important point in *qigong* exercises, it is located in the middle of the sole of the foot, in a soft depression. It is approximately one third of the distance from the toes to the heel.

CHAPTER 8

IT'S UP TO YOU TO SEEK AND REALIZE THE WAY

When most people think of Daoist practice and its practitioners, they imagine otherworldly characters from a kung-fu movie, clad in a long robe with a *taiji* symbol[1] on the front and the eight trigrams[2] on the back, holding a fan and sporting long silky mustaches flowing down to their chest. They imagine men bearing the same countenance of Zhuangzi as he stood on a bridge watching fish, his face calm with the look of one who has "returned to the truth."[3] Or else, they imagine a stalwart, stoic, and placid character who is always refining their internal kung-fu, deep in stillness. Such musings paint lions as house pets, and turn the dignified into the profane.

Throughout the course of his life—from the time he entered the Dao, seeking the Truth, to his eventual achievement of the Fruit— Ma Danyang showed no signs of affectation. Among his sayings, some had the sole purpose of warning his disciples, to wit: "Where the mind resides, there is the *qi*; when the mind scatters, one departs from the Dao." In this regard, he advocated for enveloping everything we do uniformly within the mind. This principle applies to all forms of "activity"—whether walking, sitting, lying down, or in conversation—as well as when performing Daoist rituals and practices. In other words, wherever you are and at any time, your

---

1 太極. The symbol (of two stylized fish, most frequently in black and white) representing the concept of the "ultimate supreme" in Daoism, or *yin* and *yang*. The martial art by the same name is based on this very concept, of opposite polarities entwined with one another.

2 八卦 (*bagua*). Eight symbols used in Daoist cosmology to represent the fundamental principles of reality, seen as a range of eight interrelated concepts.

3 濠上觀魚 (*haoshangguanyu*). This references a scene from the "Zhuangzi" book, a foundational text of Daoism: it outlines the carefree state of the Daoist sage.

true mind must contemplate emptiness. During seated meditation, regulate the breath until the inhalation and exhalation are even and concentrated at the tip of the nose. While in the process of falling asleep, don't forget to have your mind settled on the *dantian*: in this way, there will never be a moment when your mind is fragmented, regardless of whether you are still or in motion. This is how to train your *qi*.

To train your *qi* to the highest level is to make it seem both there and not there at once: it's being in stillness imperturbable as a mountain, and in movement swift and ungraspable as lightning. Sometimes, it is like a rabbit escaping from its den: all of the dirt and dust leave the mind and *qi*, and the breath has not the slightest coarseness. As you go about your daily life, try to avoid letting your mind get caught up on mundane things, for even the most minute of these thoughts will, in an instant, disperse the *qi* you have spent a long time cultivating. Amid all of our thoughts, true mind must emerge, a collected and whole entity that, once cultivated and brought to maturity, signals that we are not far off realizing the Dao. For beginners who are on the path of Daoist *qi* cultivation, yet still unable to do away with scatteredness of mind, do your best not to dwell on the past, nor busy yourself thinking on what is yet to come. Just focus your attention on the moment at hand and your bearing will become like a signpost visible to all, announcing: "uninvolved."

Nowadays, some present their style in a manner appearing nimble, agile as a swallow in the sky, or as if they are attempting to pass through snow leaving no trace. Some make a display of their power and seek to make off with the respect given to a charging tiger. They seek to accomplish great feats, like climbing up sheer walls, by manifesting an otherworldly speed, grace, and prowess. From my experience and study, I would say that the more accomplished a Daoist practitioner believes him or herself to be, the harder it will be to enter the innermost chamber where the entirety of the scroll and the essential instructions are unfurled. When cultivators of the past practiced the stages of "securing the furnace [lower *dantian*] and erecting the cauldron [upper *dantian*]"[4] and "entering the furnace to smelt the sword"—or any other stage for that matter—without the guidance of an experienced and accomplished practitioner, it was considered potentially very dangerous and harmful to oneself. Thinking on it, an authentic transmission is no more than a few words: if these are applied persistently and with diligence, you will see the results for yourself. The most frightening thing someone could do is buy some books and practice blindly. Masters of the past have reminded us unremittingly that the true transmission is in the words of your teacher, and there is no need for superfluous words or text. The essential instructions on internal alchemy are brief and concise: on closer inspection, you realize that many of the books on internal alchemy consist mostly of verbiage and repetition that stray away from the Dao. We should indeed be careful.

Frankly speaking, the patriarchs have revealed great secrets in many Daoist texts, yet subsequent generations of practitioners, lacking a generous mind, have covetously concealed them. Their tricks have led generations of seekers to exhaust all means searching far and wide, with nothing to show for it at the end of their pursuit. As the past masters said: "The Dao is in oneself, do not seek it far away." This phrase tells us that if you want to seek the truth and attain the Dao, the starting point must necessarily be your own flesh, blood, and bones.

There are even today some dreamy practitioners who cling conservatively to the old system and believe that once the time has ripened one shall accomplish the path by simply completing one's daily practice regiment. As early as the Wei, Jin, and North-South dynasties (220–589 CE), most of the common people practiced internal alchemy and took herbal medications, but if we were to probe further we would see that for every ten thousand practitioners, it would be hard to find but one who was accomplished—immortals such as the patriarch Lu Chunyang are

---

4   The three *dantians* are also referred to as the "three cauldrons." The more commonly referenced *dantian* is indeed the "lower *dantian*," located below the navel inside the abdominal cavity, where the process of developing the elixir by refining and purifying essence into *qi* begins. But there is also a "middle" *dantian* at the level of the heart, where spirit is stored and where *qi* is refined into spirit, and an "upper *dantian*" at the forehead between the eyebrows, where spirit is refined into emptiness.

indeed anomalies. We can thus see that most words spoken in the field are meant to dazzle and confound, and we ought to be careful not to put much store in such boasts.

CHAPTER 9

THE SECRET BEHIND CULTIVATING ESSENCE[1] AND SUPPLEMENTING *QI*

In my opinion, modern people ought to focus only on meditating every day, continuously paying attention to breath regulation, and never interrupting the daily Daoist movement practice: these are the most important conditions for cultivating health in body and mind in the modern world. Unless you're going to pass away soon, movement practice can be very beneficial for restoring lost *qi*. If you wish to follow the examples of those who have pursued the path of immortality, then you will have to make careful note of the *Dao De Jing, Can Tong Qi, Wu Zhen Pian, Huang Ting Jing,* and so on—this will be enough. In the past, having pursued the Dao for many years, I relentlessly asked numerous noble Daoist masters questions about the *Can Tong Qi* and *Wu Zhen Pian*. Since I counted myself among the dull-witted of men, the only option I had was to take great pains to repeatedly immerse myself in the *Wu Zhen Pian*, every new reading yielding new insights—though I cannot say I fully understand it yet.

The *Wu Zhen Pian* is the gold standard for Daoist practitioners on the path: its author lived in the time of the Song dynasty, and was a patriarch of the southern school of Daoism. Those who came later called him the "true achiever" of Ziyang, whereas his householder name was Zhang Boduan. Before passing the highest imperial civil service exam, he was already an erudite scholar. He was especially fascinated with, and pursued, the technique of Daoist

---

1 精氣神 (*jingqishen*). According to Daoism, energy comes in three forms: essence (精), *qi* (氣), and spirit (神). The aim of the Daoist is to transform essence to *qi* and finally to spirit.

alchemy. During his decades of holding office as a civil servant he was grieved again and again by the ways and happenings of state affairs, and early on developed the aspiration to renounce worldly life. Later, found guilty of setting fire to books, he was demoted and assigned to the southern region of Lingnan, and often roamed the Daoist temples in the Guangdong belt in search of achieved Daoist masters.

After a while, having bumped into an accomplished practitioner transmitting the Dao in Chengdu, he headed towards Hubei to practice, finally settling in Linhai, where he sat down in full-lotus and eventually obtained immortality. When his disciples cremated his body, thousands of relics[2] were obtained from his remains.

Emperor Yongzheng of the Qing dynasty had immersed himself deeply in the study and practice of Daoism and was well aware of Zhang Boduan's contribution to the Daoist canon for subsequent generations. He was also the Daoist master for whom the emperor had the greatest personal admiration, and so while enthroned the Emperor posthumously conferred on him the title of "Great Compassionate and Accommodating true man Chan Immortal of Ziyang," and had a Daoist temple erected as a memorial to him in Ziyang. The *Wu Zhen Pian* lays out a description of the spirit of internal alchemy in extensive, penetrating detail, and blends it with the thought of Laozi; the artfulness of the author's prose draws an endless stream of enraptured admiration from the reader. Anyone who really took the time to delve into the text a hundred times or more would naturally gain deep insights.

Even more so, the *Yellow Court Classic* is an ancient text which those who walk the path of the immortals must recite and apply. Due to an early hobby of mine to copy calligraphy inscriptions, I had come into possession of a manuscript version of the *Yellow Court Classic* by the brushes of Dharma Master Zhiyong, Chu Suiliang, and Zhao Mengfu. In fact, I had already recited it many times and was quite delighted by it, so it proved a very beneficial

---

2   舍利子 (*shelizi*). Generally understood in the religious context as objects intimately connected to the life of a saint or holy person. In the Daoist context, there is the added meaning of the essence of a practitioner that coalesces and solidifies into small durable beads.

practice to write it down. It is necessary for any practitioner of internal alchemy to become intimately acquainted with this text: I myself only came to understand the preciousness of the human body through reading and reciting it. Later on, while studying Vajrayana Buddhism's 100 *yidams* of the *bardo*,[3] I was astonished to learn of all the many spirits inhabiting the human body. It cannot be denied that human life is a rare gift, and every bit as real.

The idea of the human body having three *dantians* originates in the *Yellow Court Classic*, and its instructions on keeping the emotions at bay and on *cunxiang*[4] meditation are exhaustive. If studied in greater depth, you'll find it's full of some of the earliest concepts and theories of Chinese medicine. In many places, we are able to see how it was long ago understood how to direct the *qi*, how to cultivate essence, how to achieve longevity. Also, in order to facilitate the practice of subsequent generations, the text separated the human body into three parts: upper, middle, and lower.

In brief, if you are profoundly knowledgeable of Chinese culture and are familiar with the terminology of Daoism, reading the text a couple dozen times should grant you a good grasp of the practice of *daoyin* and *qi* circulation, cultivating essence and supplementing *qi*, adjusting the breath and visualizing, and so on. The *Yellow Court Classic* still stands as a text of extreme importance for modern people willing to seriously study and practice *qigong*.

---

3 中陰百尊 (*zhongyinbaizun*). Yidams are meditational deities, known as aspects of the enlightened mind. The 100 *yidams* of the *bardo* are those deities that inhabit every person and become known throughout the process of dying. These deities are also associated with practices in Vajrayana Buddhism that can purify the body and mind.

4 存想. A form of meditation, practiced by early Daoists, which relies heavily on visualization.

CHAPTER 10

RELAXING, RELAXING AGAIN
MIND AS CLEAR AS A MIRROR

Ma Danyang was the main disciple of the immortal Wang Chong-yang, and the founding patriarch of the School of Complete Reality I belong to; he initiated the transmission of this authentic tradition that would continue through many generations. It was during a rather precarious and adverse time of his well-known life that Wang Chongyang entered the path of the immortals. One day, drunken and insensible, he happened upon the immortals Zhongli Quan and Lu Chunyang, and instantly felt a deep connection to them; over time, they shared with Chongyang the oral tips for practicing the path of immortality. He then made the hard decision to leave his prosperous and comfortable household and make his way alone to Nanshan,[1] to practice austerities secluded in retreat. The initial stage of his practice was quite unusual: in order to generate a mind of renunciation and one-pointed diligence, he dug a grave ten feet deep to serve as his meditation seat, and there he would sit, day and night without interruption, practicing. It is said that during this period of time his feelings and experiences reached thoroughly penetrating depths; yet, although there were many people who followed him along the path, he was rather dissatisfied with them as potential disciples.

It was later on that he drifted over to the region of Ninghai,[2] and crossed paths with the affluent Ma Danyang and his wife Sun Buer. Ma Danyang was so inspired by Wang Chongyang that he left the home life to practice the Dao wholeheartedly, even offering up his mansion. On its grounds, the Quanzhen Temple was built,

---

1   南山. A mountainous district of Shenzhen.
2   寧海. A coastline in the East of Zhejiang province.

which became known to later generations as the birthplace of the School of Complete Reality. Taking the couple as disciples marked the beginning of the expansion of Wang Chongyang's teaching career, and the spreading of Daoist doctrine: from then on, he received a succession of disciples, future holders of the lineage of Complete Reality, with whom he was quite pleased, such as the "true men" Qiu Changchun, Wang Chuyi, Hao Datong, and others. After Wang Chongyang opened the gates to his teaching, he moved to the Kunyu mountains[3] in Shandong, where the incessant influx of students continued to grow, and his activity flourished with great vigor. It is a pity that Wang Chongyang's life in this world was short—before the age of 60, he ascended to immortality, entrusting the great responsibility of continuing the transmission of the teachings to Ma Danyang.

Wang Chongyang's impartiality in regards to other schools, and his belief that the creeds of the "three doctrines"—Buddhism, Daoism, and Confucianism—could be mutually beneficial, are the reasons I so admire the teachings of the School of Complete Reality. This ideology differs from the tenets of other southern schools and sects; he demanded of his disciples that they delve into the Classics of Buddhist doctrine—the *Heart Sutra*, the *Diamond Sutra*, the *Lotus Sutra*, and so on—and placed equal reverence on the doctrine of Confucius. If you visit the main hall of a Complete Reality School temple, it is common to see offerings presented to figures of Buddha or Guanyin on the altar. From the teachings and writings of Wang Chongyang, it is easy to discern the vestige of his single-minded investigation of Chan in his early years; he was also full of praise for the enlightened masters of all Chan schools.

He deeply believed that to awaken to the Dao and "reality" one cannot be attached to words and images, and he did not consider charms and the worship of deities to be a mandatory practice. What he placed emphasis on was safeguarding spirit, cultivating *qi*, having the stillness of a mountain, practicing good deeds on a large scale, and discreetly accumulating meritorious acts. Thus, in my early years I was heavily influenced by Wang Chongyang's thought

---

3 崑嵛山. A group of scenic mountains in Shandong Peninsula, China.

and path of cultivation, and for a very long period I engaged in the joint practice of Daoism and Buddhism.

A point that is particularly emphasized in his teachings is that of an individual's karmic obstructions: if these are not purified, even if this person could summon the winds and rains, they would still be repelled by the God of Thunder. As far as the School of Complete Reality is concerned, then, internal practice is of extreme importance.

In the less than 20 years that followed Ma Danyang and other prominent disciples taking charge of propagating the School, its tenets had already spread over every province—a resplendent page in the history of the Daoist teachings in China! I once recited verses in which Ma Danyang and his master Wang Chongyang echoed one another, which drastically enhanced my sense of blessing.

The great influence patriarch Wang Chongyang had on Ma Danyang becomes apparent in the latter's words:

> For practitioners of the Dao working on the oral tips of the Complete Reality School for meditation and *daoyin*, nothing outweighs being still and calm at all times, relaxing and relaxing again until relaxation is complete, with a mind as clear as a mirror, untainted by mundane thought. This is when achievement is at hand. Remain uncontaminated by any and all mundane connections, and the spirit and *qi* will circulate by themselves...

If readers are able to experience for themselves this heartfelt advice, they will reap wondrous and inexhaustible benefits in both their sitting and moving practices. Always remember that what all the sages, patriarchs, and men of virtue continually propagated were indeed not fancy footwork and mysterious powers and abilities, nor displays that leave the beholder forever perplexed. All is to be sought for and found only in quiet stillness and relaxation.

In the past, many fellow Daoist enthusiasts have asked me to expound on the Dao, but I am left feeling remorseful at my shallow investigation and understanding of the teachings. Indeed, I have not actualized what I learned, to say nothing of achieving great expertise, and as such have been unable as of yet to exert myself in teaching, or in deeply receiving the instruction of my revered masters. Spiritual practitioners who cultivate in secret should adopt a humble, self-reflective, and self-effacing demeanor. This is all the more true in the context of the Path of Dao—akin to the ocean, as vast as it is deep: in no way it is something that I, in my limited view and capacity, can hope to attain. Also, I plead for the magnanimity of my elders for it is only due to the insistent request of fellow practitioners for the past couple of decades that I shamelessly share—with people with a karmic connection—these slivers of knowledge and basic practices. It is not that I seek to keep others at bay; rather, it is that owing to my foolish temperament, I often get bogged down in the affairs of the world. Besides, the study of Daoism is profound, and I believe myself to be, to this day, still a student, unable in this capacity to impart the slightest abstruse oral instruction on practice. For this, once more, I pray to all saints and beings of virtue to forgive me.

CHAPTER 11

UNITING THE BREATH AND MIND FROM THE *DANTIAN*

Master Ma Danyang, in reference to practices both of stillness and movement, was always circling back to a central idea as conveyed by his teacher and founder of the Complete Reality school, Wang Chongyang. In the words of the latter patriarch: "The oral tip on meditation and *daoyin* from the Complete Reality School affirms the supremacy of maintaining the body and mind in a constant state of equilibrium." Even when practitioners have acquired a deep level of relaxation, a deeper one is yet to be achieved. Once the deepest level is attained, the mind can be observed as clearly as a mirror, free from even the smallest of thoughts. This is the moment when the efficacy of practice is proved to be accomplished: practitioners are unaffected by any external circumstances, maintaining an unfettered manner at all times.

When I was first learning posting exercises from my *sifu*, the first thing I learned was the breath. He said that regardless of what path or practice you seek within Daoism, they are all connected in a central way to the breath. Your breathing eventually needs to reach the state of "turtle breathing"[1] before you can see the power of your practice emerge. As such, *sifu* began with the method for "taking two breaths in, and one out." It really is just that: two breaths in, and one out, both from the nose. The only thing is that the length of the two in-breaths together needs to match the length of one out-breath: what you will want to avoid is exhaling too often or for too long, or taking shallow, short in-breaths. This kind of breathing actually accelerates aging.

---

1   龜息 (*guixi*). A method of Daoist breathing that involves breathing directly from the *dantian* without the need for air to pass into the lungs.

You must follow the ways of past masters if you want to learn *qigong*. Inhalations should be long, and exhalations short. I once witnessed firsthand *sifu's* demonstration of breathing from the *dantian*. After breathing in, one of his students started a timer and placed it on a desk. He left shortly after to run errands. When he returned more than three hours later, *sifu* had yet to release his breath. It seemed as if he could have held it there as long as he wanted, that it was entirely under his command. You can practice taking two breaths in, one breath out throughout your daily affairs until you get accustomed to it. From there you can move on to taking four breaths in, three breaths out. Being so unlike the breathing we've used our whole life, this method can feel a little unfamiliar at first. This is why beginners start with shorter breathing practices, and work their way up until their breath is united with their *qi*.

One thing to note here: these breathing methods should only be practiced by beginners when they are in seated meditation or the posting stance. Before reaching the unification of breath and *qi*, this should not be practiced while walking, running, or doing anything which quickens the breath. Also not recommended for beginners is meditating in the full lotus posture, which could constrict the *qi* from circulating properly. Sit upright on a bench, stool, or the edge of a bed, with the feet planted on the floor and the hands placed on either kneecap. Straighten the spine using intention, not physical strength. All other aspects of the meditation should follow the normal practice and posture. In the past, there were a few older students who had no previous experience of meditation. In their advanced years, they suffered naturally from weaker *qi* and stiff joints and bones, making it impossible for them to sit cross-legged. But after using the above-mentioned practice, over time there were a few among them who, after so many years of taking medication for sleep, were able to stop taking it altogether. Some were able to heal their ulcers without medication as well. It is safe to say that many small medical miracles occurred from their practice. It is the experience of those who do this practice consistently twice a day, one hour in the morning and one at night, that it will bring staggering changes to both the body and mind.

For most people, breathing is just an intake of oxygen that happens either through the nose or the mouth. As it is eventually utilized by the cells in the body, the path oxygen takes is normally from the bronchial tube straight to the lungs. Without vigorous physical activity, a normal, stable rate of breath for a single minute is anywhere between 15 and 19. It goes without saying that physical exertion, whether from running, walking, or transporting physical objects, would dramatically change that rate. This differs from the long-term practitioner of *qigong* or meditation. This kind of person would have already become accustomed to breathing from the *dantian*—the anchor and "control center" of the breath—rather than from the chest.

One of the fundamental skills to achieve in the practice of either posting or meditation is the deepening of the *qi* to the *dantian*. Reaching this step also brings out clear results from your training. In reality, there are volumes of breathing exercises for the human body, and the body itself contains many points for the release and absorption of the *qi*. Our pores themselves are each a gateway for "breath." If practiced correctly, any beginner can train the breath to the point where it becomes soft and fine, and the mind quiet and virtually uncluttered by scattered thoughts. This, in turn, opens up the pores and causes copious amounts of sweating. For experienced practitioners who have already completely changed the way their body functions, however, you would rarely see these kinds of effects.

CHAPTER 12

GETTING THE GIST
OF RELAXATION

In the past, during the summer months we would often have the chance to stay at the temple and serve *sifu*. As energetic and young as we were, our short-sleeved shirts would be drenched with sweat in the height of August, especially without any recourse to air conditioning or fans. *Sifu*, however, seemed completely untouched by the muggy summer weather, walking around in his long-sleeved Chinese gown. Even after going showerless for 100 straight days—and without once changing his clothes—I couldn't pick up the slightest trace of body odor or sweat standing next to him.

At one point, we asked *sifu* about this and he replied: "Going naked or taking a shower is a good way to deplete the *qi* you've built up during your training." *Sifu* said that foregoing showers for long periods of time was a habit of his from youth, when he was training in the mountains, and it didn't feel strange to him. "For practitioners whose cosmic orbits have opened and who have returned their breath and *qi* to its true, original form," he continued, "their 'nine orifices are free of scent.'" In other words, there are no odors left behind by anything expelled from the body, even after relieving one's bowels or bladder. This is made possible from daily meditation and *qi* training, inducing the body to constantly "cleanse and restore": the pores of the body are kept completely clean and open. This is in stark contrast to those who are fed too well, sweat and breathe like an ox at the slightest movement, and drag around too much meat on their bones. The difference is evident.

As skill in meditation and breathing techniques progresses, the breath begins to deepen below the skin all the way to the bone marrow. Experience has shown that the skeletal frame of people who are not in the habit of training their *qi* and paying attention to their health will show signs of aging from youth. The bones begin to deteriorate, and the marrow atrophies and enters necrosis, impacted as such by the lack of daily physical activity that supports the production and dissemination of blood (the hematopoietic function) to the body.

As mentioned above, breathing is our unbreakable tether to life from the moment we are born until the moment we die. However, some beginners might not be accustomed to the breathing of meditation and *daoyin qigong* practices, and might tighten up in the chest. This is just our internal diaphragm muscle not having acclimated to the practices yet. If you regularly use the aforementioned breathing techniques, your lungs will grow stronger, your lung capacity will increase, and the diaphragm will naturally descend. It will become second nature to contract the abdomen on your outbreaths, and after frequent repetition and the regular exercising of the diaphragm, the stuffiness and stiffness in your chest will gradually subside.

Since the importance of relaxation was covered earlier, now I wanted to touch on *how* to relax. Everyone knows the word "relax," but actually getting into a state of deep relaxation is another issue entirely.

When you are practicing the posting[1] stance, begin by planting your feet shoulder-width apart. Visualize a string running through your body, from the very center of the top of your skull all the way through the perineum and down between the legs into the ground. Your body becomes a weightless, empty balloon tethered to the string. Relax the entire body, from the hairs on the top of the head down to the *yongquan* point on the bottoms of the feet. The body becomes entirely empty and transparent. After you have repeated this visualization three times, visualize that the string running through your body is tugged upwards. Breathing in, your "balloon body" shrivels up as if its lost its air. Breathing out, you again inflate with air. Do this three times, following the breath

---

1   站椿 (*zhanzhuang*). A particular set of *qigong* methods, in which the body is kept static and in a set position, much like a post. Many examples are listed in Part II later in this book.

cycle. If you have done this correctly, you should quickly feel a significant release of any pressure and stress in your body and mind. That is the main purpose and benefit of this exercise.

After your body and mind have completely relaxed, slowly raise and open the arms up in front of you. Visualize two tiny goose eggs resting just under the *yongquan* points on the bottoms of the feet. Be careful not to squash and break them. With the body and mind emptied and alert, sink into a slight squat, keeping your knees from extending out beyond the toes. At this time, everything from your waist down should feel as if you are immersed in a pool of water: the body is buoyant, empty, and weightless. From the waist up, visualize that your arms are raised to the level of the *tanzhong*[2] and wrapped around a huge, weightless balloon. They hang in a relaxed manner with the palms facing your chest. All five fingers of each hand are facing each other, separated by a fist's distance. These are all the rudimentary points needed for beginners to learn posting.

Once you start to become familiar with these essential points of relaxation and breath and you reach a level where you are able to relax more deeply during the exercise, you can add another layer to your visualization. Visualize, in the center of the ball that you are already hugging, another *taiji* ball about the size of a baseball. You can use the following visualization to train your focus: during your inhalations, the *taiji* ball disappears; then on your exhalations, the ball reappears. Count each set of breaths until you reach ten. You can work your way towards longer breath counts as you deepen your training experience. If you are doing the exercise correctly, your body should feel warm, sweating slightly, your breath will feel gentle and even, and your mind will become more tranquil.

If you are experiencing any of the following symptoms, from a Chinese medicine perspective you might have excessive *yang qi*[3] in the body: high blood pressure; frequent faintness, dizziness and a slight sensation of swelling in the head; somewhat blurry, muddled vision; nausea accompanied by ringing in the ears; and frequent

---

2   膻中. Acupuncture point located roughly at the center of the sternum, in line with the nipples.

3   陽亢 (*yangkang*). The *yang*, masculine aspect, from the balanced dichotomy of *yin* and *yang*. Excessive *yang* (or *yin*) denotes an imbalance in the body.

dryness in the tongue and lips. Another way to check is sticking out the tongue: it will be bright red on the sides and the tongue coating will be very thin. This type of condition often points to *exuberant liver heat*. Usually this condition is accompanied by poor sleep quality, irregular drinking and eating times, and insufficient *kidney water*. A person with some or all of these symptoms should not place their attention on any points above the waist. In addition, they should divide the exercise into three-to-five-minute segments and intersperse each segment with the relaxation exercise. Whenever possible, they should place their attention on the goose eggs visualized under the feet.

CHAPTER 13

NATURAL AND UNCONTRIVED

THE ESSENTIALS FOR RELAXED POSTING

When it comes to relaxation while posting, one ought to bring awareness to the *dantian* area as the focal point and then, based on your physical condition, you can either perform actions to replenish or purify the body.

To replenish, take a deep breath and visualize the *qi* performing an orbit along the governing and conception channels (also known as the *Ren* and *Du* channels). While you are doing this, visualize that the air you breath in is utterly pure and beneficial to all your organs. Though shapeless and formless, this *qi* is in accord with your intention and contains the purity, truth, and benevolence from between Heaven and Earth as well as the best of the five elements.[1] This air subsequently permeates and travels through the governing and conception channels as well as the eight extraordinary vessels (also known as the eight extraordinary channels) before migrating to the rest of the body.

To purify, exhale and visualize that you expel all illnesses and deep-rooted turbid *qi* hidden in the darkest corners of your psyche. You should visualize the turbid *qi* sinking into the ground in front of you, going into the deepest reaches of the Earth never to be found again.

In this way, continue alternating between in-breaths and out-breaths. Accompany the visualization with a basic relaxation exercise—completely relax the whole body from head to toe. If you haven't got the hang of this exercise, you may have your mouth slightly open during the out-breaths and while still breathing out

---

1   五行 (*wuxing*). The Five Phases or five elements—metal, wood, water, fire, and earth—that make up the physical universe, according to ancient traditions. They were later used in traditional Chinese medicine to explain various health conditions.

through the nose you can visualize the body relaxing all the way down to the *yongquan* point. On the exhalation, gently enunciate the syllable "ha." After practicing like this several times, you should feel a lot more grounded and relaxed.

For those who experience discomfort in the stomach and intestines, before doing the relaxation exercise, bring awareness gently to the discomfort and follow the same "ha" exercise, visualizing the discomfort leaving with the exhalations and sinking deeply into the ground. If you have a basic understanding of Chinese Medicine, or even better understand acupuncture, you may place awareness on the acupuncture points related to the discomfort and expel the turbid *qi* out of the body into the ground during exhalations. For those who feel that they have poor circulation or metabolism, they can do one to three repetitions of the *qi* moving exercises concerning the governing and conception channels, along with the rest of the eight extraordinary channels and 12 channels, in order to complement the relaxed posting practice. However; if you feel tired to the point of not even having the energy to talk or your body feels heavy and awkward, then in order to avoid further exhaustion it's best not to repeat the exercise too many times.

For novice practitioners of the relaxed posting practice, the general principle is to avoid forcing yourself to practice for a long period of time; instead, all sequences should be done in a natural, non-forced way. Those with more experience with this practice, whenever aches and pains occur, are able to relax the whole body from top to bottom, section by section. In areas where discomfort is present, they would press the areas with both palms while focusing on the out-breaths (to expel the discomfort) several times. According to practitioners' accounts, most will then experience a sense of relief and restored comfort.

Visualizing the path of relaxation (in your body) is only needed during exhalations. It is not necessary to do so during inhalations: just imagine that what you inhale and absorb is pure and beneficial *qi*. This is the basic requirement of the "cleansing and restoring" stage. If you are more on the sensitive side, it is suggested that you have your eyes open while doing the relaxed posting practice:

indeed, people who are more sensitive or prone to being nervous and who tend to keep their eyes closed during the practice, may shake and tremble due to irregular flow of *qi*. However, if you are the active, brash and careless, impatient type, find it hard to settle down, and have coarse breath, then you can choose to keep your eyes closed while inhaling and exhaling. All in all, there are over 100 methods for posting, 12 of them more commonly practiced. Whatever method you choose, the general principle is to utilize proper breathing and attain complete relaxation throughout the body.

CHAPTER 14

A POST A DAY KEEPS
THE REAPER AWAY

In recent years, it seems that a great number of martial artists have begun promoting posting with a vengeance. According to Daoist masters of the past, however, real posting was explained as early on as the *The Yellow Emperor's Internal Classic*,[1] which was completed in 26 BCE. Chapter 1 contains a passage:

> In ancient times there were true men
> who could extract the essence of heaven and earth,
> grasp the principles of Yin and Yang,
> attain pure energy through the breath,
> guard their spirits with great care,
> the physical body seamless with the Way.
> Their spirit spans ever on,
> the length of heaven and earth,
> aligned with the spirit of the Dao.

This paragraph very clearly explains that, if you are able to understand the ways *yin* and *yang* work in the body, and, using this knowledge, combine it with breathing practices, then you will reach the state of unifying the essence and spirit. In ancient times, there were a great many accomplished Daoist practitioners who relied only on breathing: they practiced "exhaling the old and inhaling the new," as well as *daoyin* and the transformation of essence into *qi*, and then, of *qi* into spirit. Finally, they would go back to the spirit and void between Heaven and Earth, a level where the physical body has attained complete transformation.

---

1 黃帝內經 (*huangdineijing*). An ancient Chinese medical text regarded as the fundamental doctrinal source for Chinese medicine for more than two millennia. Composed of two texts, each of 81 chapters.

Therefore, the phrases in the *Yellow Emperor's Internal Classic* that state "muscles as one" and "the physical body is one with the Dao" explain that if someone understands posting, single-pointed focus, breathing and *daoyin*, eventually they may be able to unify their physical body with Heaven and Earth and become everlasting as the sky.

Once, when I was talking with an old Daoist priest about posting practice, he mentioned Wang Yuyang, a figure among the patriarchs of the School of Complete Reality. Later generations referred to him as Yu Yangzi, the founder of the *Yushan* school. He learned under the guidance of the achieved practitioner Wang Chongyang and received many important oral tips from him. He even received an imperial invitation to expound on the path of immortals to the emperor. The emperor offered a set of dark magenta Daoist robes to Yuyang; his refusal did not diminish the high regard in which his cultivation and virtue were held. At any time, he could be seen with flocks of hundreds of followers.

It is said that Wang Yuyang had his own unique posting practice. He would stand with one foot raised, doing the stance on a single leg. After nine years of vigilance in his one-legged practice, he achieved the Supreme Dao. There are a great many past patriarchs and venerable practitioners who achieved success through posting—so many that their number is too great to cite one by one. However, regardless whether you are a cultivator of the Daoist path or a martial arts practitioner, those who practice the true *qi* cultivation[2] can all reap unbelievable benefits from diligently practicing posting.

Starting with *Zhang Sanfeng* onwards, many *taiji* schools have sprouted, and I have heard many names for various posting practices: *taiji zhuang* (*taiji* posting), *sanyuan zhuang* (lit. three dollars posting), *jianglong zhuang* (lit. descending dragons posting), *fuhu zhuang* (lit. subduing a tiger (overcoming sinister forces) posting), and so on. As I was particularly fond of martial arts from an early age, I studied internal schools of martial arts,

---

2   養氣. In Daoism, the conservation of vital powers is achieved by avoiding conflict with the unchangeable laws of nature. Also a Confucian concept of fostering the spirit of nobility (by moral cultivation or through a moral life).

external schools of martial arts, weaponry, as well as the way of the sword. All of these have their own merit. Regardless of which martial arts tradition you are studying, posting practice can, in all cases, serve as a foundation. The "Yellow Emperor's" *Nanjing*[3] also talks about the principles of *qi*. In fact, you can obtain this same understanding from posting practice. Regardless of whether you are using medical treatment or life-nourishing techniques from the *Daoist Canon*, the goal is always to clear away all stagnant blood and blockages in the channels that have accumulated over a long time. It must be noted that, if one does not take drastic action to use these types of curative methods, then all illnesses will still continue to afflict the body. Therefore, you should use posting practice not only to consolidate the root and cultivate the original *qi* but also to activate and enrich the essence, *qi*, and spirit. According to the experiences of previous generations of practitioners, daily practice of posting will prevent any turbid *qi*[4] from afflicting the body. You don't need to spend any money, you only need to rely on breathing. Given the benefits, surely it is worth the effort.

In the past, during a period of learning *taiji*, I heard that during the decline of the Manchurian Qing dynasty, within the great imperial palace, there was a figure named Yang Luchan. From an early age, he practiced martial arts and posting. On freezing, snowy days, any snow within a foot of his body would not reach the ground but rather naturally melt in the air. His body would not touch a bed, and he would rely only on posting. Eventually, he even developed the ability to push *qi* through the air. With regards to pushing *qi* through the air, I have heard about and personally seen several practitioners who had this ability. One of these practitioners would stand on the fourth floor of a building and control people three floors below. He could use the *qi* in the air to force his students on the bottom floor to shout and fall to the ground.

---

3   難經. One of the major books used in Chinese medicine. Written in the 1st century CE, it focuses mostly on the Yin Yang and the *Five Phases* (see note 1, Chapter 13) and their application both in theory and medical practice. It offers what was at the time considered an innovative way of approaching needle therapy and pulse diagnosis.

4   邪氣 (*xieqi*). Any of six pathogenic factors that could invade the body causing problems: wind, cold, heat, toxins, dryness, or dampness.

Another expert was able to use the moment between breaths to seemingly create a protective sphere around him. None of his students could step into the sphere and touch him. If they tried, they would be swept to the ground by a wave of *qi*. There was also a senior who, when an opponent attacked him, would lift his hands as if handling a bow and arrow, and the opponent would be shaken by a great force. I saw as he made the sound "ah" that people behind him would be pushed back about three meters, just like dirty laundry. However, they would not be in the slightest way injured. Apparently, in their youth, these skilled experts were diligent in foundational posting practices and this diligence led them to develop such abilities. All this doesn't even begin to speak to the value of posting nowadays in order to maintain health, gain peacefulness, and achieve longevity. For all of these benefits, posting is, obviously, a very important foundational practice.

CHAPTER 15

Effortlessly Achieved Fetal Respiration

The Natural Arising of True *Qi*

Generally speaking, in regards to physical fitness, the purpose of meditation is to soothe the internal organs and nourish and restore the essence, *qi*, and spirit. A step further is to then include the practice of the microcosmic and macrocosmic orbits.[1] However, it is well known among experienced practitioners that a foundation of posting combined with breathing methods like exhaling the old and inhaling the new (to purge impurities) can, over time, also clear the channels of the entire body. You may also come to realize that the efficacy of posting exceeds that of sitting meditation, and that, in regards to smoothing the flow of *qi* and blood, results are quickly seen. The reason is that beginners of seated meditation often have stagnation of *qi* and blood in the lower abdomen and in their crossed legs. Therefore, a long time is needed to dredge the channels and disperse the stagnation. It's important to have unwavering perseverance in this approach. Additionally, if you are not yet 50 and have never sat in the lotus posture or have never done seated meditation before, then beginning with seated practice may require much more stamina and perseverance than you are willing to expend. Therefore, I usually recommend starting from the relaxed posting practice in order to strengthen the body. Starting in this way is often more beneficial than directly doing the sitting meditation practice.

The preceding book in this series, *Climbing the Steps to Qingcheng Mountain*, introduced some important points about posting.

---

1   小周天,大周天 (*xiaozhoutian, dazhoutian*). Daoist practices that involve moving the *qi* through channels in an "orbit" around the body.

Along with the basic posting methods, there are some tips we can incorporate into the practice. When posting, after relaxing the body, you return your attention to the mind by focusing on a single point. For example, visualize that in front of your chest, you hold a large balloon in your arms. In the center of this balloon is a *taiji* ball about the size of a fist. In order to keep the mind on a single point of focus and avoid being disturbed by people, responsibilities, things, or sounds in the external environment, just focus your attention on the two fish of the *taiji* for the time being. When inhaling, clearly visualize the eyes of the two fish closing tightly, and when exhaling, clearly visualize the eyes of the two fish opening wide. The fish are vivid and lifelike in appearance, and move continuously with the breath. Practice this regularly and over time your mind will become still and calm.

This exercise is used if the mind is easily distracted during practice, preventing the *qi* from entering the lower abdomen area around the navel. Also, pay attention to the air moving in and out of your nose. You should hear no sound. If you are able to hear your breath, then this is not true breathing and it means your internal *qi* is scattered. Or perhaps there is no sound, but between the nostrils there is an uncomfortable, dry, and sluggish sound. This is indicative of *qi* being stuck (not flowing freely) somewhere in the body. Ultimately, you must practice until the breathing is completely silent and undetectable—the in-breath arrives without a sign and the out-breath leaves without a trace. This is the moment when *yin* and *yang* naturally balance, the bones support themselves, the true *qi* naturally arises, and fetal breathing is naturally accomplished.

Those beginning the practice of "relaxed posting with regulation of the breath" should try to bring the *qi* down to the *dantian* when inhaling, and when exhaling let the *qi* rise up from the *dantian* and then exit through both nostrils. After becoming familiar with this method, and practicing over time, you will begin to develop abundant and unimpeded *qi*. This is the starting point for later achievement of fetal breathing. In the past, when I practiced this and arrived at the end stages of the exercise, I would stick extremely thin pieces of cotton paper over the nostrils. The requirement I set,

CLOUDS OVER QINGCHENG MOUNTAIN

was that on exhaling, the cotton strips would not fall down. What is the reason for this? It was to develop the ability to breathe in and out through the umbilical (navel) area instead of the lungs, nose, or mouth. A long period of time devoted to practice is required before you can take a deep breath and hold it in the umbilical area, in the *dantian*. Silently count in your mind from one to ten to begin with. Then try holding the breath for a count of up to 21, then try 100, and so on. When exhaling, you must make the breath so subtle as to be virtually non-existent, and the main priority is to make sure the cotton doesn't fall from your nose.

While practicing this, also pay close attention to the temperature of your breath. This is because the temperature of your breath can reveal the state of your internal organs. More experienced practitioners don't need to rely on the pulse to make a diagnosis— from the temperature of the breath they can tell which areas of the body need to be repaired or revitalized. In the past, I often heard the elders talk about old masters who could hold a single breath for ten days. They would inhale a single breath of air, draw it into the *dantian*, and wouldn't need to take another breath for a week or more. I also heard about a Daoist practitioner who sat in meditation on the bank of a stream. When he inhaled, the stream would stop moving, and when he exhaled the water would again murmur and flow.

CHAPTER 16

THE YELLOW COURT BREATHING PRACTICE[1]

USING INTENTION TO CIRCULATE *QI*

Once you've gotten to a certain point in your relaxed posting practice you can move on to the Yellow Court Breathing Practice. To be more precise, this method is to be practiced after your initial relaxed posting. Once in the posture, focus is placed below the navel. But you must begin first by guiding the body to relax using intention: starting from the crown of the head, breathe naturally and relax all the way down to the *yongquan* acupoint. Do this seven times before moving into the main breathing practice. Breathe in and imagine the *qi* descending slowly to the *dantian*. Don't overexert yourself when you're still unfamiliar with the practice. Once you feel that you are able to control the movement of your *qi*, you can hold the breath once your *qi* has reached the *dantian*. This is not to be done forcefully, or you might find you start to involuntarily run out of breath. With the breath still under control, let it out slowly. Repeat this exercise 7 or 21 times.[2]

A warmness or faint vibrating sensation in your *dantian* at any point during this phase of the practice is a sign of proficiency, and means you can progressively lengthen the amount of time you hold the breath in the *dantian*. This should be segmented, for example, by extending your held breath for gradually longer periods of time, from one minute up to ten. It is important that you do not rush or

---

1   黃庭呼吸法 (*huangtinghuxifa*). "Yellow Court" here is a reference to a Daoist or TCM anatomical term for the human body, specifically the torso. It's an analogy to the organs of the body being like an imperial court, with their specific rank and function, i.e. ministers and kings, etc.

2   This breathing exercise should not be practiced if you are experiencing any problems related to the heart, blood pressure, or psychological illness.

force your breathing at any point—it should always remain fine, soft, and even. Once it loses these qualities you've gone beyond your (current) limit.

Once you've progressed to the point where your breath comes less from the nose and more from the *dantian* itself, you're ready to practice "breathing through the back." You can couple these movements with your posting practice, while still in control of your breath. When you breathe in, slowly raise the hands from the sides up to the level of the eyebrows, all with the palms facing the sky. On the out-breath, let the hands sink until they reach the level of the *dantian*. Fold the hands, one over the other with the thumbs interlaced, and press them lightly against the area of the *dantian*, drawing the stomach back towards the spine. Breathe naturally, seven times. Once you've done this exercise enough, you should be able to be suck the breath all the way to the spine without the aid of the hands, though you shouldn't try and force the stomach into this position. Once you've finished the set, end it with the closing exercise. Return to a natural breathing pattern, just making sure that your eyes are halfway closed, and that your focus is on the *dantian*.

CHAPTER 17

PURE AND CLEAR *QI* DIRECTLY ENTERING THE *DANTIAN*

There seems to be a wide spectrum of posting practices and specific areas of focus; however, having studied under six different masters, it is my humble opinion that the similarities outweigh the differences. Sometimes the focus is on the *dantian*, or on the *tanzhong* point, or perhaps on the *mingmen* or *huiyin*.[1] However, beginners shouldn't be in a hurry to focus on specific points. Putting attention on adjusting the breath is more appropriate.

When you have adjusted the breath, you can begin to move your attention, and then begin to focus on specific points. In other words, if you focus on the *dantian* too soon, forgetting to adjust the breath, you will skip a fundamental step. Furthermore, if the foundation is established then the breathing can be forgotten and there will be a sensation of vibration coming from the *dantian*. When this happens, your opportunity is ripe and it is the right time to focus on points during posting.

Generally speaking, regardless of which point you choose to focus on, you must first understand the practice of "cleansing and restoring." Begin by inhaling and exhaling three times. Imagine the turbid *qi* moving from the head down to the *yongquan* point. Take another breath and move the turbid and diseased *qi* of your body out from the *yongquan* point, and deep into the earth. Continue until it all disappears, but keep your attention resting on the *dantian*.

Keep up with these fundamental practices, repeating them until they've become familiar and your mind and body are thoroughly

---

1   命門, 會陰. The *mingmen* is the "gate of vitality," an important point in the lower back between the kidneys, on the same horizontal level as the lower *dantian*. The *huiyin* refers both to the area of the perineum and to an acupoint located near its center.

relaxed. Then proceed with the simple exercise of "Gathering the Clear and Discarding the Turbid," as follows.

Even the ancient Daoist practitioners abided by these same fundamental oral tips and slowly obtained the marvels within. When breathing, use your intention and don't use force. When inhaling, curl the tongue upward and lightly press it against the upper palate behind the teeth. Keep your teeth together and don't allow any air to leak from the mouth. The reason for curling the tongue up is to allow the spirit and *qi* to descend down to the *qihai*[2] point. Over time, this will greatly benefit the kidney *qi* and kidney water. Focus your attention entirely on the *baihui*[3] point on top of your head, as though you had a large bowl balanced there and feared it falling off and breaking. The *baihui* is the governor of all the body's *yang*. All the acupoints of the body as well as the skeletal system connect to it. The three major channels also converge here. Arrive at a natural state; both eyes reflecting back the light, and your spirit will not leak out. Keep the eyes open, but don't force them. This will benefit your whole body, your spirit, and your *qi*. Relax the lower back, but don't try to force it: feel as if you are loosening your belt, and suddenly your waist opens up, allowing *qi* to circulate unencumbered.

In short, the myriad forms of posting all adhere to the same principle, which is relaxation. Body, mind, and spirit should be absolutely void of the slightest use of force. Using force will create tension, which will cause *qi* to stop in its path and stagnate. When *qi* stagnates, the mind and spirit become chaotic. In posting practice, one thing to avoid is tilting the head back. This may cause the lower back to collapse or to push the knees too far forward. The secret lies in the curvature of the spine/waist. Regardless of which practice you do, you need to pay close attention to the tips of your ten fingers, allowing a slight amount of intention to reside there. If you are practicing martial arts, the opening and closing of the pores is crucial. In posting practice, the pores must harmonize with your respiration. On the inhalation, tightly close the body's pores. On the exhalation, relax slightly, but don't open the pores completely

---

2   氣海. An acupoint located between the belly button and *dantian*.

3   百會. An acupoint located at the crown of the head.

in order to keep the wind and cold from entering the body. Keep to the principle of long inhalations and short exhalations. The in and out of the breath should flow smoothly, like the Yangtze River, moving to the sea without interruption. Listen closely to your breath until you infuse yourself in quiet emptiness. When inhaling, take the purest and cleanest *qi* from between heaven and earth, and put it into the *dantian*, as was spoken of previously.

If you practice posting diligently every day, basically, after three months you should have tangible results. Gradually, between breaths, the hands and feet will have a sensation of fullness. The palms of the hands and soles of the feet will also feel hot. After continuing to practice for a time, some people will even begin to have this same sensation of fullness in their ears, head, and sinuses. Often they may feel some kind of fullness or wriggling sensation that slowly extends from the head down to the waist. When you begin to have these kinds of sensations, it means you have reached the basic entry level of posting practice. You are ready to continue and may ask your teacher for further instruction.

CHAPTER 18

PRACTICING THE *TENDON TRANSFORMATION CLASSIC*

TO TRANSFORM THE TENDONS AND BONES

The first *Tendon Transformation Classic* I acquired was a thread-bound, privately published edition gifted by my teacher. From that point on, to facilitate my practice, I collected information relating to this book wherever I could. During this time, I looked through more than a dozen versions, varying from wood-block prints to hand-written ones. I also read a version that was just a translated summary of a Buddhist text called the *Marrow Washing Sutra*. This version even included the phrase "Thus have I heard, once the Buddha told Subhuti..."[1] I found this reference baffling, almost laughable. Another copy I came across was the edited version of the translation of Bodhidharma's[2] Classic by Pramiti (a legendary Indian monk who travelled to China). Later on, when I was learning the internal martial arts (from the Wudang school) including *xingyi*[3] and *bagua*, I was also gifted two books from the master: *The Meaning of the Tendon Transformation Classic* and *Introduction to the Practices of the Tendon Transformation Classic*. All in all, I reviewed scores of variants of Bodhidharma's text.

---

1   Although "Thus have I heard..." is a standard opening phrase in Buddhist *sutras*, it is misplaced (at best) at the beginning of the *Marrow Washing* text manual mentioned. The author is lightheartedly commenting on the difficulties encountered, even then, trying to find legitimate transcriptions of ancient texts, what with the trove of unofficial copies of doubtful provenance.

2   達摩 (*Damo*). A 5th- or 6th-century Buddhist monk from India responsible for bringing Buddhism to China. He became the First Patriarch of the Chan (Zen) school of Chinese Buddhism, and compiled the *Tendon Transformation Classic* (易筋經 *Yijinjing*).

3   形意. A martial arts system that translates approximately as "Form-Intention Fist," or "Shape-Will Fist."

According to some, the *Tendon Transformation Classic* was actually written by the Daoist practitioner Zi Ning. Regardless of authorship or how many versions of the 12 exercises of the *Tendon Transformation Classic* there may be, if we look only at the exercises, the movement of *qi* along the channels, and the breathing techniques involved, none poses a threat to health or the internal organs, which is reason enough to not pay too much attention to the exact provenance of the book: what actually matters are the physical training and the health benefits of the exercises themselves. As for the ancient myths and legends of the various lineages, I don't feel the need to explain these in great detail. Therefore, over time when asked by fellow practitioners and students about this subject matter, I have always maintained a fairly neutral and non-argumentative attitude.

In fact, those who actually studied the exercises from the *Tendon Transformation Classic* know that their transformative nature is the main reason they are so highly valued. According to numerous ancient texts and Daoist scriptures, breathing techniques involved in these exercises enable practitioners to guide their *qi* to positively affect the blood, which subsequently transforms the essence, which in turn transforms the bone marrow. If you diligently practice these exercises on a daily basis, within nine years the effort will pay off and the transformation of tendons and bones will be achieved, as evidenced by the consistent results achieved by past Daoist practitioners. Seeking ways to preserve essence, move *qi*, transform blood, strengthen bones, and be free from aches and pains, Daoist practitioner Zi Ning and other predecessors put a lot of thought and effort into integrating and compiling the ancient health-promoting exercises and marrow-washing methods of successive generations, as well as the various styles of *daoyin* exercises. These time-honored ancient physical exercises naturally have their merit and value for humanity.

From a very young age up till now, I have learned eight variations of the *Tendon Transformation Classic* and marrow-washing methods with different masters. I deeply feel that practicing the *Tendon Transformation Classic* exercises is the least time-consuming and hassle-free way to really achieve both mental and physical well-being in this modern age. Furthermore, it's entirely risk-free. The benefits, to name but a few, include strengthening the channels and bones, developing fine breathing patterns, and balancing the *yin* and *yang* aspects in all areas of your life. Many fellow *Tendon Transformation Classic* enthusiasts in their sixties and seventies manage to maintain their muscular strength and firmness, as well as their bone density. Some of them, who used to catch colds three to four times a year, can go for ten years without catching one. This allows us to ascertain that the practices indeed fortify the immune system. What's more, according to many elders and senior practitioners, the *Tendon Transformation Classic* exercises help in dealing with long-term insomnia, dysautonomia, insufficiency of kidney water, problems related to reproductive organs, cardiovascular diseases, imbalances in the digestive systems, joint problems, ailments pertaining to poor blood and *qi* circulation, as well as various other conditions.

Of all the masters I learned *Tendon Transformation Classic* from, at least two are centenarians, yet they never displayed signs of aging or frailness, and instead always maintained an upright posture. There was no arching of the shoulders and spine, or any lack of coordination, tremor, or weakness of the limbs. Quite the contrary, they had strong and sonorous voices, were graceful in their movements, and would frequently take hikes up mountains. Youngsters would not outdo them. They had smooth skin with minimal vein lines, few wrinkles, luminous but rosy complexions, bright eyes, clear minds, and astounding memories. I believe this is all related to their decades-long practice of the *Tendon Transformation Classic*!

CHAPTER 19

RELAXING THE BODY
HARMONIZING THE BREATH

The *daoyin* practices within the *Tendon Transformation Classic* are a bit different from other exercises. This lies in how the effect of stretching, lifting, and breathing is carried out in the four limbs, the muscles and joints, the sacrum, and the flow of blood. When doing the exercises, it is important to be mindful and unhurried. Just be natural, slowly and calmly aligning the breath with the movements. Following these steps is a reliable way to achieve deep relaxation of the muscles, nerves, and joints. To this end, a little pause between changes in the posture goes a long way in furthering that relaxation. If you're too tense, move too quickly, or forcefully pull, lift, and twist, in some cases you can subtly damage the nerves. In the worst cases you could sprain muscles. This makes it necessary to begin the exercises by first relaxing the whole body inside and out—the tendons, muscles, nerves, joints, and bones—and then clearing your head of anxious thoughts or apprehension about the future. In fact, keep your mind free of any thoughts if you can, staying in the moment. Steady and adjust your breathing until it feels comfortable. Don't be uneasy, don't be agitated, and don't rush.

There is a method *sifu* once taught me to use when unsure of my own ability to get into a truly calm and relaxed state. Imagine a slice of cheese sitting on the top of your head. While having no warmth of its own, the cheese nonetheless begins to melt and slowly slides down, filling your whole body until you feel nice and relaxed. If you want, you can also try visualizing a rainbow, the kind that appears after a storm. The light slowly descends, relaxing you as it fills your body. Or try another one: imagine yourself floating in a pool, completely absorbed and relaxed in your solitude. Regardless of what method you use, the first signs of your body relaxing might be a feeling of fuzzy numbness, the same way you might feel as you close your eyes to doze off for an afternoon nap. When this physical sensation comes, imagine the *qi* moving slowly from the top of the head down to the *yongquan* points on the bottom of the feet. Coordinate the movement of the *qi* with your inhalations and exhalations. When you become proficient in the exercise, you will notice that your breath becomes so slight as if it's not there. From here on you will have tangibly better results with any of the exercises you practice from the *Tendon Transformation Classic*.

Tendon Transformation Classic practices are mostly done from a standing position. Before you begin the actual exercises, you should take your body through the preparatory exercise first. Place your feet shoulder-width apart and relax each part of your body from head to toe, looping through until your breathing becomes natural and everything down to your organs and cells is fully unwound. How do you know if you've genuinely relaxed? Run a self-examination, beginning from the crown of the head. If the area in and around your brain is truly relaxed, you'll have noticeably fewer thoughts, especially the anxious worries that normally buzz around. You'll feel similar to how you would in the moments after snapping out of a dream. Gradually move your examination down your face towards your throat and nape of the neck. Feel as your throat becomes smooth and comfortable. Feel happiness seeping into your body. Continue downward to your chest and back. Feel that they are as broad as the ocean and open as the sky. Feel the *dantian* and the kidneys filling and replete with essence and *qi*. Continue downward from the perineum all the way to the *yongquan* points, relaxing the inner, outer, and lateral parts of the upper legs as your awareness passes through. There is an unspeakable feeling of something gently flowing all the way to the *yongquan* points, something bringing deep relaxation and comfort. Jumping back up to the crown of the head, you can relax the entire body again: through the eight extraordinary channels, the twelve organ channels, to every organ and every last spot, inside and out. After finishing the self-suggestions composing this relaxation cycle, you will be officially prepared to begin the 12 *Tendon Transformation Classic* exercises.

CHAPTER 20

RELAX THE GROIN, SINK INTO THE POSTURE

In the earlier years of my practice, I would normally couple the practice of internal *taiji* with the "open arms body relaxation exercise." I would also weave in a set of exercises from the *Tendon Transformation Classic* to the beginning and ends of this long string to boost the effectiveness of the exercises. All of these *qigong* exercises come through the health cultivation practices passed down by Zheng Huaixian, who received them from Sun Lutang. If you practice them meticulously, you will experience their uncanny power for yourself.

At an even earlier period, I also practiced for a long time the Six Harmonies and Eight Methods, or Water Fist for short. The set originates with the old master Wu Yihui. If you can combine it with two basic practices *wei tuo gong*[1] and 3 Divisions, 12 Spirits,[2] you can set a foundation for your internal and external *qigong* stronger and denser than the roots of an oak tree. When I was practicing the internal martial arts intently, I melded the heart practice of the Water Fist into my training. Once I had practiced the forms until they flowed with unfettered grace, I was able to appreciate the deeper meaning and quality of the "full body" *jing* and the "twining silk" *jing*.[3] Through these movements, lithe and unpredictable like a dancer's gait, I felt a sensation running up and down from crown to

---

1   韋馱功 (*weiduogong*). A standing meditation, one of five internal forms of the Six Harmonies and Eight Methods.

2   三盤十二勢三 (*sanpanshiershisan*). One of six hand forms in the system of the Six Harmonies and Eight Methods, including three sections and 12 forms: Dragon, Phoenix, Tiger, Crane, Leopard, Ape, Bear, Goose, Snake, Hawk, Roc, Kylin.

3   整體勁, 纏絲勁 (*zhengtijing, chansijing*). *Jing* (sometimes spelled *jin*) is an unseen, intangible force or power, without form or shape. In *taiji*, the "full body" *jing* refers to all the body's power and energy being condensed into an exploding, surging force; whereas the "twining silk" *jing* is an elastic repelling force that activates against attacks to the body.

feet and permeating me completely, as if each pore of my body was a weapon, repelling and deflecting anything that came close.

In the past, in the midst of my captivation with the internal and external forms of martial arts, I slowly gained an experience of the mind's relationship to posting and *daoyin*. Especially for beginners in posting, when practicing the basics, under no circumstances should you jump ahead and omit relaxation. From start to finish, pursue truth by way of real experience.

You must undertake your practice with no fear for numbness, soreness, or pain. Regardless of whether you are practicing meditation, *daoyin*, martial exercises or posting, from the very beginning, everything has its own logic. As the saying of *taiji* grandmaster Yang Chengfu goes: "If one fails to suspend the head and relax the neck, one's three decades of practice are in vain." This very principle, of having the head stand straight with a relaxed neck, applies equally well to the posting.

Although relaxation is emphasized in the practice of posting, from beginning to end there should be a certain feeling. Just in the way that a native of India might be able to balance anything on the top of his head, essence and *qi* naturally fill the entire body. So when the whole body really becomes completely relaxed, essence, *qi*, and spirit will naturally, and without obstruction, traverse the entire body.

Why is it that the shoulders must be relaxed? By way of intention, when the shoulders are thoroughly relaxed, the spirit and *qi* are directed to the elbows and then to the palms of the hands, and finally to all of the fingers. At this time, both hands are lifted into a circle (in front of the chest). *Qi* from the posting practice naturally returns and enters into the *dantian*, then the chest and upper and lower back also relaxes. Once the lower back relaxes, the governing channel will be freed of any stagnant *qi*. At the same time, the *qi* is very easily led to the conception channel, at the front of the chest. We absolutely must not neglect all the minor details of the posting practice, which all have their purposes.

Apart from this, if you train in martial arts and moreover have practiced *xingyi, bagua,* or *taiji*, then you will be able to sense the importance of the waist and hips. Whether it is for posting, horse stance or push-hands, if you are not able to relax the hips, then the lower body will not have the steady and stable feeling that the heels and soles of the feet are like a deep network of intertwining roots sinking into the ground.

Furthermore, if you have practiced *xingyi* or *bagua*, then you understand the importance of the relationship among the tailbone, *dantian*, and *mingmen*. If you can practice to a point of connecting the actions of these three areas then you will have access to an unbroken flow of *qi* and energy. The bend in the knees should be determined by your stability and your ability to withstand an external force, because, from the perspective of martial arts, the knee and the back of the hip are in the state of pushing and pulling to maintain the stability of the body. However, if this is in the practice of *qigong*, this method should not be employed as it will cause a break in the flow of *qi*. Actually, in internal martial arts, posting, and especially *xingyi* and *bagua*, the focus is at the *laogong*, *yongquan*, and *baihui*. The soul of the foot needs to be stable, connected to the floor. The ten toes are closely held together. Relax your awareness as well as your body's essence and *qi* completely, all the way down to the *yongquan* points. If this method is put to proper use—especially as mentioned in the *Classic of Kungfu* (*Quan Jing*) concerning the origin of strength coming from the legs—and *qi* comes from the legs, is controlled by the hips, and followed by the shoulders and fed into the arms, naturally there will be a limitless well of strength bubbling forth.

CHAPTER 21

MOVING *QI* TO THE FINGERS WITH *TONG BEI QUAN*[1]

The *Tong Bei Quan* also has its foundational training methods, but it involves yet again a different style of posting. This practice is of great benefit to the joints, muscles, nerves, spirit, and internal viscera.

The basic practice method of *Tong Bei Quan* is called "Silent Standing Six." This method originated in Hebei province in the western mountains of Beijing, and was brought to Taiwan by a Daoist master by the name of Han. It contains the essence of *Taijiquan*,[2] according to the innermost teachings of the founder of the Yang style, Yang Luchan. If practiced in tandem with seated meditation, there will be great complementary benefits.

Actually, as far as foundational exercises are concerned, this drill is very simple for beginners. Stand with your feet shoulder-width apart, the soles of the feet even on the ground, knees slightly bent and turned slightly inward, but lightly turn the hips out to either side. Use your intention to slightly tuck the tailbone forward, and let the spine naturally lengthen without using force.

Hollow the chest and straighten the back. Relax the shoulders, letting them sink towards the earth and naturally droop down. Put your attention and your body weight directly onto the hips. Relax your neck, slightly tuck in the chin, and keep the tongue on the roof of the mouth. Fix your eyes on a point about three feet in front of you, keeping them half open and half closed. The base must be stable and sturdy, while everything above the hips should remain empty and weightless.

---

1   通臂拳. A kung-fu style that uses long, whipping arm movements and whole body integration.

2   太極拳. As previously mentioned, the martial art form based on the principles of the *taiji*. Also known as TaiChi.

The mind should have no thoughts of the future or the past, only focusing on the breath. At the start of the practice, take a breath from the *dantian* and, making the sound "ha" with your mouth, eject all the dirty *qi* from the body and all delusive thoughts from the mind. After this, breathe in and out only through the nose.

While inhaling, guide the *qi* down to the *dantian*. While exhaling, lead the *qi* out of the nostrils.

Avoid using force while you breathe, keeping the breath natural. Relax while you inhale, letting the chest expand outward and drawing the *dantian* in. Let the chest relax while you exhale, allowing the *dantian* to extend forward. Thirty-six repetitions count as one round.

For the sake of brevity, I will only explain one of the many practice methods here. Carrying on from the previous section, after completing your practice session, lift your arms up to the sides of your body until they form a straight line, with the palms facing downward. It is important to keep the shoulders completely relaxed while doing this, and have a sinking sensation internally. At this point, use force to spread outward from the shoulders to the joints of the arms and hands. Then move the *qi* from the joints of the back out to the palms using some force. At this point, extend the fingers out horizontally and imagine they are extending infinitely to the left and right, feeling as if there was a person on either side of your body helping to pull your hands to the sides. After completing this exercise, begin to inhale. When inhaling, expand the chest, draw the abdomen inward, and lift the perineum slightly. Guide the *qi* to a point about one fist's distance below the *tanzhong* point. At this point, gently exhale through the nose, relax the chest and abdomen, and sink the *qi* into the *dantian*. By means of inhaling and exhaling, push the *qi* and intention down the arms to the fingertips. When done correctly, this exercise will produce a sensation of swelling, tingling, and warmth in the arms, palms, and fingers. Repeat the action of extending and retracting for a minimum of 36 breaths. The wonderful thing about this exercise is how it allows you to harmonize yourself with the *qi* of Heaven and Earth, and how it fills the entire body with energy; your *qi* and blood will circulate smoothly. In the end, you will acquire the ability to move your spirit and *qi* without hindrance to the fingertips.

The methods of *Tong Bei Quan* have proliferated over time. There are the Five Elements, Six Harmonies, and *taiji* styles of *Tong Bei Quan*, as well as *Pi Gua*, *Tong Bei*, and Two Wings styles. However, they all come from the Shaking Root, Rushing Shoulder, and Flinging Wrist arm drill foundational exercises.

The principal function of this practice is to make the hands like iron rods, the wrists like sponges, and the arms like whips. By combining the breath with extension of the body, the heart and lung function will also benefit greatly. Furthermore, twisting the waist back and forth, along with posting, will stimulate the *qi* and blood to penetrate into the ankles, heels, and directly to the *yongquan* point. Relaxing the shoulders and extending the arms naturally allows the acupoints of the shoulders and arms to naturally open. The *qi* and blood will flow unobstructed throughout your life, and prevent any kind of problems from developing in your cervical vertebrae, shoulders, or arms.

There are, of course, many principles to take note of in this practice. In *Tong Bei Quan*, if one develops proficiency with the drills, a certain kind of strength is developed. All the power originates in the lower spine, raises up the back and passes through to the arms. It takes only a hint of intention to move the *qi*, which is immediately transferred to the fingertips. There is no strength used in the arms, and in an instant the power is flung outward a specific distance. It is an effect I have witnessed many times, not just with the aforementioned technique but also with chopping, throwing, and slapping. The myriad schools of *Tong Bei Quan* are all the same. *Qi* is sent from the waist, moves up the spine, through the back, then passes through the shoulders to the arms where it manifests as many different techniques like piercing or drilling. The primary focus is to make the hand like a lance and the arm like a whip, with speed like a meteor shooting through the arm.

CHAPTER 22

TAIJI BREATHING AND PRACTICES

UNBLOCK THE CHANNELS

Taiji body relaxation breathing techniques can also be used when doing posting or exercises from the *Tendon Stretching Classic*. The *taiji* body relaxation breathing techniques use breathing together with *daoyin* and with the addition of upward and downward flow of *qi* (both innate and acquired) one is able to get to the stage where *qi* flows in an unobstructed way. With frequent practice, it is possible to prevent illness; when incorporated with meditation or *taiji* practice, it is possible to balance internal *qi*, stretch the muscles and joints, and smooth out the energy channels as well as boost strength.

The method is very simple: when doing *qigong* practice, feet stand shoulder-width apart, the two legs naturally relax and the groin sinks back. However, you must pay attention to your tailbone, and suggest to yourself that it flips slightly to point backward. In this way you can allow the soles of your feet to be firmly planted on the ground. The spine should be relaxed but straight, and the lower jaw and chin should be slightly tucked in. Once again, observe yourself. The *baihui* point at the top of the head should be perfectly in line with the perineum, with the base of the continuing line hanging down between the feet, which still stand shoulder-width apart. Those new to the practice should remember to not let the neck reach forward. The head should be kept straight with the tongue pressed to the upper palate. The eyes look straight ahead, the shoulders are relaxed, the arms droop down, the elbows are drawn slightly apart to the left and right, while the palms face backward and the fingers are kept relaxed and ever so slightly apart. After completely settling into this position, practice the breathing: on the inhalation, the tongue is pressed lightly against the top gums; on the exhalation, the tongue pushes slightly against the lower gums. Other actions are to be matched to the in-breath and out-breath: on each inhalation, all the muscles of the body should be tensed slightly and the perineum should be lifted slightly as well; however, this is done using intention not force. The tongue is pressed against the top gums and the eyes are kept open looking attentively forwards. On the out-breath, close the eyes a little, drop the tongue down to the lower gums and relax all the muscles from the face to the *yongquan* point and the perineum, and repeat this seven times, until the body is comfortable and the palms are tingling with *qi*.

When doing this practice, you must remember the guiding principle of keeping the whole body relaxed. The exhaling of the old and inhaling of the new, the coming and going of the breath, should be completely natural, and the smoother and finer the better. The breath cannot be forced or held, otherwise this could lead to cramping or other side effects of improper practice. Depending on a person's health condition, on inhalation they should try their best to simultaneously suck the stomach in and bring the *qi* to stick to the back. This can awaken the *taiyuan*[1] point. Over time, the "original breath" (innate primordial *qi)* will naturally arise. This point is also where the veins and arteries meet. By using these kinds of breathing methods we can naturally activate the eight extraordinary channels thereby causing all of the channels in the body, big and small, to open up without obstruction. On inhalation, constrict the perineum slightly using intention rather than force. The perineum is extremely important for both men and women, as it is the hub from which life begins; the male prostate gland as well as other related organs are all connected to the area around the perineum, so through breathing, exhaling the old and inhaling the new, one can greatly benefit the energy and functions of the whole body. Regarding what was mentioned earlier about sticking the *qi* back to the spine when inhaling, the "back" here

---

1   胎元. An acupuncture point about 4.3 cm below the belly button, important in establishing one in fetal breathing.

includes the coccyx, sacrum, *mingmen*, lower back, *jiaji*,[2] and the spine all the way up to the *yuzheng*.[3] All of these points are on the back of the body. Often through inhaling and exhaling, one can exercise the pathway of areas on the back, no matter whether it's regarding the governing and conception channels or the circulation of *qi* and blood, among many things. The effects are tremendous.

---

2   夾脊. An acupuncture point about halfway up the spine, also called the *huatuo's* paravertebral points, located about 0.5–1 cun lateral to the depressions below the spinous process between T1 and L5.

3   玉枕. "Jade pillow," an acupuncture point on the back of the head.

CHAPTER 23

LONG-LIVED IMMORTALS

TRUE *QI*, TRUE BREATH

Throughout the course of China's long history there have appeared a large number of great practitioners who achieved outstanding longevity, living to grand old ages like tortoises. Their life spans, seemingly limitless as the sky, resulted from a combination of good fortune and realization of the oneness of meditative stillness and wisdom. Of course, for them the matter of *qi* was easy. For example, the figure of the past known as Peng Zu obtained the art of breathing from the immortal Yin Shouzi. Peng Zu then lived in seclusion on Mount Wuyi in Fujian province, where he would practice all day long. When he finally came down from the mountain, all of his old friends were amazed by his youthful appearance and healthy, strong figure. He was repeatedly approached by people questioning him on health cultivation. He answered by saying, "All the time conserve your vital powers and use the water cassia flower [Chinese water cinnamon], grind muscovite [a kind of mica—a crystal mineral found in rocks] into a powder, add deer antler and take as medicine." He said nothing else. But it's commonly said that he was merely an official scholar at the time, was able to marry repeatedly, gaining a number of wives, and still was as light and graceful as a swallow. He had dazzling skin with a clear and rosy complexion and his movements were as quick and nimble as the legendary *Jiao* dragon that controls rain and floods. He was also as strong as a fierce tiger. If it were not for true *qi* and ever-present true breath, then how could he have accomplished this?

In the time of China's Wei, Jin, and North-South dynasties there was a person known as Bei Du[1] (lit. cup cross) who was

---

1   杯度. A legendary monk known for being a bit of a maverick figure, who conducted himself in a rather unpredictable manner.

even more spectacular. One time he stayed as a guest within a family home. The family venerated a noble, gold plated statue of the Buddha. The more he saw it, the fonder he became of it. On the day he left, without saying a word to his hosts, he took this Buddha statue with him. Seeing as the statue had been passed down through generations, how could the family simply leave the matter at that? Mounting horse-drawn carriages, they pursued Bei Du. They hounded him in earnest and could see him walking casually in the distance, yet even with four powerful horses gasping for breath they were somehow unable to catch up to him. The chase led them all the way to the banks of the Yellow River, where Bei Du simply took out a wooden cup from the sack on his back and cast it on the river. He stepped on the cup with both feet, took one breath and then was across the river at once. His pursuers could only stare blankly from across the river as he walked away. In his mercy, Bei Du would often take all the money offered to him by disciples and use it to buy fish and release them into the water. He had only to see a person fishing and he would get their fish from them. Often people would play tricks on him and give him fish that were already dead. But Bei Du would take the fish in his hands, blow over it and when the fish touched water again, it would come alive and swim away, leaving no trace. He would often play with the fishermen. Occasionally, the fishermen would angrily refuse to hand over any fish and would fly into a rage, trying to catch Bei Du to beat him up. If so, Bei Du would simply pick up small stones from the roadside and blow on them, before tossing them among the fishermen. Two stones would transform into a wild raging bull that would fight the fishermen. He would then destroy the fishing nets on the boats and the fish would be released into the sea. On realizing this, the fishermen would be enraged and surround him to beat him up but he would quickly disappear from sight. Bei Du is a historical figure who existed and, apart from what's described in these legendary stories, also made many accurate predictions and exhibited supernatural powers on various occasions.

There was a certain miraculous practitioner of the Dao who appeared in the final years of the Han dynasty. His name was She

Zheng. It was said that this practitioner had a thorough knowledge of all the anecdotal stories of all the successive dynasties and rulers. Even more special than that was the fact that nobody had ever seen him open his eyes. Even when handling regular daily affairs, his eyes would remain closed. There was a student who had been following him for nearly 30 years. One time the student couldn't take it anymore, so he kneeled on the ground and begged to be able to see his teacher's eyes open, but once he opened his eyes a sound like thunder continuously rolled down from the sky. The eyes were as bright as torches, like lightning! In his fright, the student could only crouch there on the ground. Later, She Zheng gained fame and his home became as busy as a marketplace owing to the large number of his followers. At one point, some of his long-time students asked about health cultivation. He revealed his daily habits of paying attention to diet and breathing, adjusting the breath, practicing *daoyin* exercises and focusing on the cultivation of *qi*. All sexual activity should be stopped and certain medicines must be ingested. After using his methods and practicing like this for many years, many others also achieved fantastic results.

Accounts of wondrous past events relating to the *daoyin* practices of cultivating *qi* or longevity and events involving supernatural changes are incalculably vast in number. Some people have cultivated their *qi* to the extent that if they lie naked in the snow, then the snow is unable to be in contact with the body (melting away). If any people come to look then there will only be the sound of thunderous snoring. In the time of the Han dynasty, the Han Emperor Wu and Wei Shuqing had a predestined (karmic) relationship. The emperor was amazed that Wei Shuqing had a face like that of a seven-year-old child. But in the end this connection was not to be. The emperor had deep regrets about this, and later could only seek out Wei Shuqing's son Du Shi. In the end Wei Shuqing left the world without a trace. According to legend, Du Shi later dug up an old box from under the family residence. The box had been buried there by Wei Shuqing and was full of resplendent mica of various colors. Du Shi lived in accordance with the oral tips of his father, adopted a specific fasting method involving ingesting mica and finally even ascended to immortality.

In ancient times, there was a character named Huang An who practiced the cultivation of *qi* and *daoyin*. It was said that he lived for over 10,000 years, yet he maintained the physical appearance of a child. He spent most of his time naked and had no need for clothes. Whenever anyone would see him, he would always be sitting on the back of a large tortoise.

Out of curiosity, many people would ask him how long he had been sitting on the tortoise. He would reply by saying, "This tortoise will extend its head out of the shell once every 2000 to 3000 years. In the long time that we have been together, I have only seen it do this five times." Emperor Wu of the Han dynasty, liked to travel around collecting extraordinary people to work for him, so he regarded Huang An with great respect. Huang An also shared many breathing and *daoyin* techniques with Emperor Wu. After the death of the emperor, Huang An disappeared from the face of the Earth without leaving a trace. No one knew where he went.

I really enjoy collecting books about the ancient immortals and studying or hearing about their stories. From this I have learned all about the great deeds of successive generations. After reading one of these stories, there will always be some kind of formless boost to my own current practice of *daoyin*, meditation, or posting. Although the stories already mentioned are just a few snapshots from a larger selection, my hope is that all those with a karmic connection will find some comfort in these stories while engaging in their own meditation or long posting practices.

Owing to meditation, practice of the teachings from every school of internal martial arts, the long time spent searching for great teachers from the three schools (of thought) as well as inquiries with countless numbers of great masters, I was never abandoned by my venerable late teachers. I am deeply indebted to my kind master from whom I received the various martial arts techniques of great teachers such as Yang Banhou, Wu Jianquan, Sun Lutang, Zhou Jinghai, and others. However, owing to dullness of wit and idleness, I did not make true progress. All is owing to the blessings and merits that have been passed down through the lineage and the great teachers who held the torch of the ancient teachings taking them into the future, as well as their tireless zeal and patient instruction. I hold this work aloft as a tribute, although I am aware that it merely offers an incomplete, fleeting glimpse of a much bigger picture, thus I beg for forgiveness and understanding.

PART 2

DAOYIN—
TECHNIQUES

SECTION 1

POSTING FUNDAMENTALS

CHAPTER 24

Posting Relaxation Exercises

Benefits of posting include: promoting the smooth flow of *qi* and blood, methodically harmonizing the breath, and clearing the channels of the entire body.

Stand with your feet shoulder-width apart, imagine a string hanging straight down from the upper *dantian* (near the pineal gland) to the *huiyin* point (the perineum), and landing on the floor between your two feet. Next, imagine your whole body as a bag of air, as if you were completely hollow. At the same time, relax your body; from the hair on your head down to the *yongquan* points at the bottom of the feet. Everything is totally empty, like a transparent crystal ball. Relax your body in this way and repeat the visualization three times.

CHAPTER 25

Posting Relaxation Visualization

Basic Posting Gazing Method

With a soft gaze, focus the eyes on a point about one to three feet in front of you.

Imagine a string attached to the top of your head, pulling you upward. On the inhalation, imagine your body as a balloon deflating; while exhaling feel that your body expands like a balloon being filled.

Do this with the breath three times.

If practiced properly, you will reduce the stress on your body and mind, and feel totally relaxed.

CHAPTER 26

POSTING 1: SIMPLE FUNDAMENTAL

FIGURE 26.1   FIGURE 26.2   FIGURE 26.3

FIGURE 26.4   FIGURE 26.5

FIGURE 26.6   FIGURE 26.7   FIGURE 26.8

FIGURE 26.9

Step-by-step instructional text

1. Stand with your feet shoulder-width apart (see Figure 26.1), relax the body from head to toes (refer to the relaxation technique in Chapter 24). Bend your knees, making sure they do not go past the toes, put your attention on the *dantian*, and keep the legs loose (Figure 26.2).

2. Move the arms outward evenly left and right, palms facing forward (Figure 26.3). Inhale and bring *qi* into the *dantian*, and focus your awareness there as well. Bring the arms to the front of the chest, in a circle, as if hugging a big tree, fingertips pointing at each other, one- or two-fists'-width apart, just in front of the *tanzhong* in the middle of the sternum (Figure 26.4).

3. Exhale and extend the arms out left and right again with palms facing forward (Figure 26.5). Repeat steps 3 and 4 three times while relaxing the whole body, from the hair on the head to the *yongquan* at the bottom of the feet.

4. Bring the arms back to the front of the chest as if holding a big tree, the ten fingertips pointing at each other, one- or two-fists'-width apart, the center of your two hands in front of the *tanzhong*. Relax your mind, and let the breath gradually come and go as it will, without any distraction and emotions (Figure 26.4).

5. With a soft gaze, focus the eyes on a point about one to three feet in front of you. Inhale and feel the *qi* coming from the *yongquan* up to the lower *dantian*, through the spine up to the *dazhui*,[1] then curl the tongue up to rest against the point where the palate meets the upper teeth (Figure 26.6).

6. Exhale and place the tongue behind the lower teeth. Repeat the inhalation-exhalation cycle up to 21 times.

7. Closing exercise: Turn the palms facing down, relax the hands by the sides of the body (Figures 26.7–26.9).

Note: The *tanzhong* is in the middle of the sternum, at the center of the imaginary line connecting the two nipples.

---

1 大椎. Acupoint of the Governor channel, on the nape of the neck, near the first thoracic vertebra, T1.

CHAPTER 27

POSTING 2: FLAT HORSE POSTURE

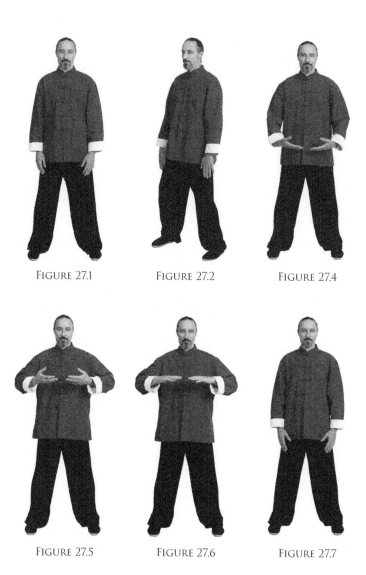

FIGURE 27.1   FIGURE 27.2   FIGURE 27.4

FIGURE 27.5   FIGURE 27.6   FIGURE 27.7

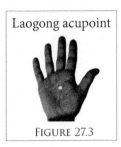

Laogong acupoint

FIGURE 27.3

Step-by-step instructional text

1. Stand with feet shoulder-width apart (see Figure 27.1), relax the body from head to toes (refer to the relaxation technique in Chapter 24).

2. Bend the knees slightly, without going past the toes, put your attention on the *dantian*, keep the legs relaxed. Let the arms hang at both sides, palms facing back. With a soft gaze, focus the eyes on a point about one to three feet in front of you (Figure 27.2).

3. Place your attention on the *laogong* acupoints (Figure 27.3), inhale and feel the *qi* coming from the *yongquan* up to the lower *dantian*, through the spine leading to the *dazhui*, and bring your tongue up to rest on the upper palate.

4. Exhale and bring the tongue down to rest behind the lower teeth. Repeat the inhalation-exhalation cycle up to 21 times.

5. Closing exercise. Palms facing up (Figure 27.4), lift the hands up to the *tanzhong* (Figure 27.5), then turn the palms down and bring the hands to rest by the side (Figures 27.6 and Figure 27.7)

CHAPTER 28

POSTING 3: SUPPORTING HEAVEN AND EARTH

FIGURE 28.1   FIGURE 28.2   FIGURE 28.3

FIGURE 28.4   FIGURE 28.5   FIGURE 28.6

FIGURE 28.7   FIGURE 28.8   FIGURE 28.9

FIGURE 28.10

Step-by-step instructional text

1. With the feet shoulder-width apart, relax from head to toe (see Figure 28.1) (refer to the relaxation technique in Chapter 24).

2. With eyes half-open, half-closed, fix your gaze on a point one to three feet in front of you. Place the palms of both

hands facing upward. Raise the hands until they are level with the *tanzhong* (Figure 28.2).

3. Turn one hand palm up and raise upward, turn the other hand's palm down and press downward. Turn the fingers inward (Figure 28.3).

4. Reach the hand raising upward to the sky; push the hand pressing downward toward the Earth, fingertips turned inward. Keep all ten fingers relaxed and spread out (Figure 28.4).

5. When your hands begin to feel sore and tingly, and you cannot endure it anymore, switch hands (Figures 28.5–28.7).

6. Repeat steps 3 to 5. You can adjust the number of repetitions based on your physical ability and available time.

7. Closing exercise: Bring the hands back to the level of *tanzhong* and then turn the palms downward (Figures 28.8 and 28.9). Relax and let the hands slowly fall back alongside the body (Figure 28.10).

Note: It is acceptable to raise either hand first.

CHAPTER 29

POSTING 4: PUSH THE WALL

FIGURE 29.1   FIGURE 29.2   FIGURE 29.3

FIGURE 29.4   FIGURE 29.5   FIGURE 29.6

FIGURE 29.7   FIGURE 29.8   FIGURE 29.9

FIGURE 29.10

Step-by-step instructional text

1. With your feet shoulder-width apart, relax from head to toe (Figure 29.1) (refer to the relaxation technique in Chapter 24).

2. Keep the knees slightly bent and place your attention on the *dantian*. Don't let the knees go past the toes. Relax the

groin area. With eyes half-open, half-closed, fix your gaze on a point one to three feet in front of you. When you inhale, raise your hands up to your chest (Figures 29.2 and 29.3).

3. When you exhale, the palms face outward and push forward at a 90-degree angle to the arms (Figures 29.4 and 29.5).

4. Inhale, turning the palms to face upward, and bring the hands back to the body (Figures 29.6 and 29.7).

5. Continue moving the palms inward along the body and then downward, pressing down toward the ground as you exhale (Figures 29.8 and 29.9).

6. Repeat steps 2 to 5 a total of 21 times.

7. Closing exercise (see Chapter 29).

Note: When pressing forward, the arms do not need to be completely straight, but the wrists should be bent to 90 degrees. Push the wall forcefully.

CHAPTER 30

POSTING 5: SECRET SWORD POSTING

FIGURE 30.1

FIGURE 30.2

FIGURE 30.3

FIGURE 30.4

FIGURE 30.5

FIGURE 30.6

FIGURE 30.7

FIGURE 30.8

FIGURE 30.9

FIGURE 30.10

FIGURE 30.11

FIGURE 30.12

FIGURE 30.13

FIGURE 30.14

FIGURE 30.15

Step-by-step instructional text

1. Stand with feet shoulder-width apart, relax from head to toes (Figure 30.1). Refer to the previous Posting Fundamentals: Posting Relaxation Exercises (Chapter 24) to relax. The arms hang naturally, inhale and exhale seven times to regulate the breath.

2. With eyes half-open, half-closed, fix your gaze on a point one to three feet in front of you. Keep the knees slightly

bent, place your attention on the *dantian*. Don't let the knees go past the toes. Relax the hip area. Your hands make the "Secret Sword" form (Figure 30.2).

3. Holding the fingers in the Secret Sword shape as you inhale, the fingertips face each other and the hands rise to shoulder height (Figures 30.3 and 30.4).

4. While exhaling and holding the Secret Sword shape, point the fingertips up (Figure 30.5).

5. Push out to the left and right until reaching full extension, pause for a moment (Figure 30.6).

6. While inhaling, hold the Secret Sword shape, the fingertips are pointing out and the palms face up (Figure 30.7).

7. Slowly return the hands to the chest, (Figures 30.8 and 30.9). Then turn the palms so the Secret Sword tips face each other (Figure 30.10), move down to the *dantian* (Figure 30.11). Repeat steps 3 to 7, a total of seven times.

8. On the seventh repetition, at the end of the last exhale, the Secret Sword hands open (Figure 30.12).

9. Closing exercise: The palms face upward, move both hands inward toward the chest (Figure 30.13), then turn the palms over (Figure 30.14) and move them all the way down. Relax and let the arms hang alongside the body (Figure 30.15).

SECRET SWORD FINGERS

The index finger and middle finger press together and extend. The ring finger and pinky are bent, and the thumb presses on the fingernails of the ring and pinky fingers.

CHAPTER 31

POSTING 6: PUSHING THE EARTH

FIGURE 31.1   FIGURE 31.2   FIGURE 31.3

FIGURE 31.4   FIGURE 31.5

Step-by-step instructional text

1. Stand with feet shoulder-width apart, relax from top to bottom (see Figure 31.1) (refer to the relaxation technique in Chapter 24 to relax.)

2. Keep the knees slightly bent, place your attention on the *dantian*, and don't let the knees go past the toes. Relax the groin. With eyes half-open, half-closed, fix your gaze on a point one to three feet in front of you.

3. The arms are straight, the center of the palms facing the ground, the fingers relaxed and spread wide. Imagine they are gently covering the surface of the Earth.

4. When you inhale, imagine *qi* is moving up from the *yongquan* points and entering the *dantian*, then moving up the spine all the way to the *dazhui*. During the inhalation, the tongue rolls up and presses against the upper palate; on the exhalation, the tongue rests just behind the bottom teeth. Inhale and exhale like this 21 times, or adjust the number of repetitions based on allowed time or physical condition (Figure 31.2).

5. Closing exercise: The hands rise, palms facing upward (Figure 31.3), then turn to face downward (Figure 31.4), finally relaxing the arms along the sides of the body (Figure 31.5).

Note: When spreading the fingers open, don't use force or tension.

CHAPTER 32

BASIC VISUALIZATION FOR POSTING

GATHER THE PURE AND EXPEL THE IMPURE

Step-by-step instructional text

1. As you breathe in, imagine all of the positive, pure, and joyous energy of the world taking the shape of a clear ball and entering into your body, going straight down to the *dantian*. From the *dantian*, this energy then spreads throughout all of the body's meridians, including the eight extraordinary meridians and 12 channels.

2. Imagine this clear energy soaking and replenishing every cell of the body, like water irrigating a dry field.

3. As you breathe out, imagine all of the negative energy you've accumulated from sickness and mental ailments over the years as a ball of dirty energy that ascends from the *dantian* and is expelled through the nostrils. It exits the body as a mass of coal-like smoke, and you send it deep into the Earth until it disappears from sight and can never be found.

> Once you've become more skilled in the practice of posting, you can add this "Gather the Pure and Expel the Impure" visualization form.

SECTION 2

BODHIDHARMA'S *YIJIN JING* (*TENDON TRANSFORMATION CLASSIC*)

CHAPTER 33

Preparation

FIGURE 33.1   FIGURE 33.2

Step-by-step instructional text

1. Stand with the feet shoulder-width apart.

2. Stand straight, hips pushed slightly forward, toes all placed on the ground.

3. Keep a straight spine, with the *baihui* and *huiyin* aligned vertically.

4. Raise the tongue up to rest on the upper palate, just behind the teeth.

5. Focus the eyes on a point about three feet in front of you.

6. Relax the shoulders with the arms hanging by the sides and palms facing backwards, fingers extended.

When beginning to practice, make sure you inhale through the nose (bring your tongue up to rest on the upper palate), and exhale through the mouth (no need to bring the tongue down to rest behind the lower teeth). As a general rule, unless noted otherwise, when practicing *Yijin Jing*, always inhale through the nose and exhale from the mouth, regardless of whether the breathing is natural, or if you inhale bringing the belly in.

CHAPTER 34

PRESSING PALMS AND HEELS UP

FIGURE 34.1   FIGURE 34.2   FIGURE 34.3

FIGURE 34.4   FIGURE 34.5   FIGURE 34.6

FIGURE 34.7   FIGURE 34.8   FIGURE 34.9

FIGURE 34.10   FIGURE 34.11

Step-by-step instructional text

1. Stand with feet shoulder-width apart, relax the body and breathe naturally. Regulate the breath and inhale *qi* into the *dantian* (Figure 34.1).

2. Inhale while lifting both heels off the ground. With palms facing up, raise the hands up to and in front of the chest (Figures 34.2 and 34.3).

3. Exhale and turn the palms to face downward, fingertips pointing forward. Push the palms down with some resistance. At the same time, lower the heels back to the ground. (Figures 34.4–34.6).

4. Repeat steps 2 and 3 a total of 21 times.

5. Closing exercise, *shougong*. With the palms facing up (Figure 34.7), lift the hands up to the *tanzhong* (Figure 34.8).

6. Turning the palms facing down (Figure 34.9 and Figure 34.10), relax and place the hands back on the sides of the body (Figure 34.11).

Benefits: Strengthens your palm and your arm muscles, readjusts and lengthens the spine, promotes flexibility and elasticity of all the muscles in the body through proper methods of inhaling and exhaling, preventing atrophy and aging.

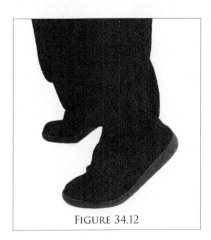

FIGURE 34.12

Lift your heels off the ground when you inhale.

CHAPTER 35

STANDING VICTORIOUS

FIGURE 35.1   FIGURE 35.2

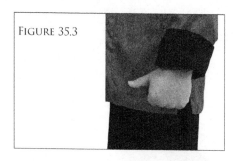

FIGURE 35.3

FIGURE 35.4

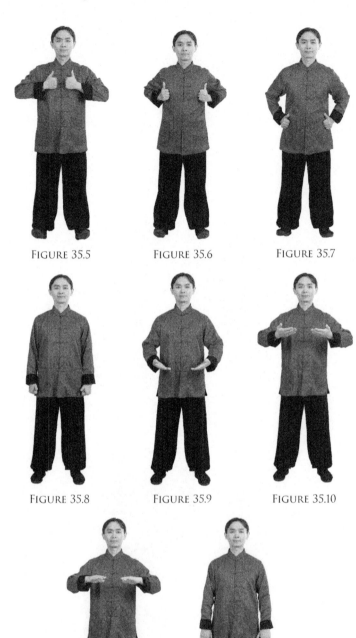

FIGURE 35.5   FIGURE 35.6   FIGURE 35.7

FIGURE 35.8   FIGURE 35.9   FIGURE 35.10

FIGURE 35.11   FIGURE 35.12

Step-by-step instructional text

1. Stand with your feet shoulder-width apart, have your thumbs extended, like a thumbs up, with the other four fingers clenched (Figures 35.1 and 35.3).

2. With your two heels strongly pressing into the ground to support the body, inhale and lift your hands up, thumbs pointing upward, while slightly contracting the anus. Supported by the weight of your heels, lift your toes (Figures 35.2 and 35.4).

3. Keep inhaling and bring your hands in front of the chest. (Figure 35.5) Press your wrists into the chest while also pushing the chest outward (Figure 35.6).

4. Exhale and slowly slide the wrists to the sides of your chest down to your thighs and stop there, while placing the soles of your feet back on the ground (Figures 35.7 and 35.8).

5. Repeat steps 2 to 4 a total of 21 times.

6. Closing practice, *shougong*. With the palms facing up (Figure 35.9), raise them up to the *tanzhong* (Figure 35.10). Turn the palms facing down (Figure 35.11) and bring your hands back to the two sides of the body (Figure 35.12).

Benefits: The movements of expanding the chest, stretching the shoulders and slowly lowering the hands can improve unpleasant symptoms such as chest pain caused by sitting and lying down for too long, as well as help the circulation of *qi* and blood in between the heart, lungs, and liver. They also enhance the body's natural antioxidant activity.

CHAPTER 36

Solid Grip with Bent Knees

Figure 36.1

Figure 36.2

Figure 36.3

Figure 36.4

Step-by-step instructional text

1. Start with the legs shoulder-width apart, arms resting at the sides (see Figure 36.1).

2. Breathe in through the nose and clench the fists, pointing the "tiger's mouth"[1] acupoint away from the body (Figure 36.2).

3. As you breathe out, slowly bend at the knees while sticking out the stomach and keeping the fists clenched. Sink the *qi* into the *dantian* as you do this (Figure 36.3). When you've completely expelled your breath, forcefully fling the fists open and stretch the fingers in an open palm.

4. Repeat steps 3 and 4, for a total of 21 times (Figure 36.4).

5. Finish the practice with the closing exercise (refer to Chapter 34).

Benefits: This exercise can strengthen the *dantian*, aid stomach and intestinal function, promote bowel movements, and increase the strength of your knee joints and fingers.

Tip: Forming a fist: tuck the thumb into the palm and wrap the other four digits around it.

---

1 虎口 (*hukou*). Located on the webbing between thumb and index fingers.

Tip: When you've completely expelled the breath, forcefully fling the fist open and extend the fingers.

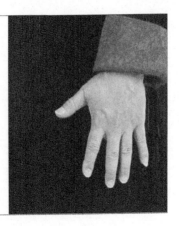

CHAPTER 37

COIL/RECOIL BODY AND KNEES

FIGURE 37.1   FIGURE 37.2

FIGURE 37.3

Step-by-step instructional text

1. With the feet spread shoulder-width apart, extend the arms out to the sides with the palms open and facing forward (see Figure 37.1).

2. Exhaling, let the stomach expand outward and slowly bend the knees. Tense the arms and legs slowly as you draw your clenched hands together at the level of the chest, all the while continuing to bend the knees lower (Figure 37.2).

3. Inhaling, suck in the stomach while releasing the tension and returning to an upright, open position with the palms open (Figure 37.3).

4. Repeat steps 2 and 3 for a total of 21 rounds.

5. Finish with the closing exercise, *shougong* (see Chapter 35).

Benefits: This form is a full-body workout. It can strengthen the muscles, ligaments, and nerves, including those of the arms, hands, fingers, calves and thighs, the vertebrae, and all the joints of the body. It also combats physical aging and prevents osteoporosis.

Tip: The key to this exercise is alternating between full body tension and relaxation. When you are constricting the body, everything needs to tense—all the muscles and joints. Then everything must release and relax, fully.

CHAPTER 38

ACHIEVE EXCELLENCE

FIGURE 38.1

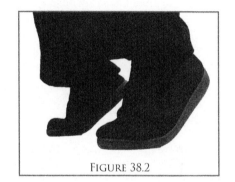

FIGURE 38.2

FIGURE 38.3

FIGURE 38.4

FIGURE 38.5

Step-by-step instructional text

1. Stand with feet shoulder-width apart, both arms extended upward, behind the ears, with the "tiger's mouth" acupoint facing behind you (see Figure 38.1).

2. Inhaling, raise your heels (Figure 38.2). Clench your hands tightly into fists, then open and extend them into the air, as if flinging something into the void. Draw the stomach in and make your eyes big, continuously staring at the space in front of you (Figure 38.3).

3. After a brief pause, exhale, and place the heels back on the ground. The hands stay raised and are once again forcefully clenched into fists; the abdomen comes back out and the eyes relax (Figure 38.4).

4. Inhaling, raise the heels, open the hands performing the releasing action into the void above, contract the abdomen, make the eyes big and continue staring into the void (Figure 38.5).

5. Repeat steps 3 and 4 a total of 21 times.

6. Do the concluding exercise (see Chapter 34).

Benefits: Through this exercise you can increase the body's energy, and gain an uplifting boost. Also, by raising the heels, contracting the anus, inhaling and exhaling, and lifting the arms and muscles of the whole body upward in the releasing action, one can stimulate and activate the 12 meridians and channels.

Note: As the arms are being raised, the elbows should not be completely straightened out or extended.

CHAPTER 39

COLLECTING THE WHOLE BODY

FIGURE 39.1   FIGURE 39.2

FIGURE 39.3   FIGURE 39.4

Step-by-step instructional text

1. Stand with feet shoulder-width apart and place the hands in front of the chest (see Figures 39.1 and 39.2)

2. Inhaling, expand the chest and open the hands, palms facing forward, arms on either side of the chest. Press the heels into the ground and lift the toes (Figure 39.3).

3. Exhaling, slightly bend the knees and place the feet firmly on the ground. Cross the arms, bending the elbows and making fists in front of the chest (Figure 39.4).

4. Repeat the movement 21 times.

5. Finish the practice with the concluding exercise (see Chapter 34).

Benefits: This practice can benefit the bladder channel and all of its associated organs. It is also a good exercise for arms, shoulders, wrists, and fingers.

Note: When crossing the arms, it makes no difference which arm is on top.

CHAPTER 40

TIME TO TURN

FIGURE 40.1   FIGURE 40.2

FIGURE 40.3

Step-by-step instructional text

1. Stand with feet shoulder-width apart and spread the arms out to the right and left. Forcefully make fists with both hands, with the palms turned up (see Figure 40.1).

2. Inhaling, draw in the lower belly. Without moving the upper arms, rotate the fists so the palms face down (Figure 40.2).

3. Exhaling, rotate the wrists and hands in the opposite direction, directing the palms up once again (Figure 40.3).

4. Repeat steps 2 and 3 for a total of 21 repetitions.

5. Finish with the concluding exercise (see Chapter 34).

Benefits: This movement will mobilize and maintain in good working condition the arms and related channels, also strengthening related muscles and parts of the nervous system.

Note: The focus is on the rotation of the wrists: keep the upper arms immobile.

CHAPTER 41

COORDINATED EFFORT

FIGURE 41.1   FIGURE 41.2

FIGURE 41.3

Step-by-step instructional text

1. Place the feet shoulder-width apart. The arms are evenly placed along the sides of the body, palms facing forward (Figure 41.1).

2. Exhaling, expand the belly outward and begin to squat slightly while the arms move in front of the body, hands clenching into fists. While squatting, tense the muscles of the thighs (Figure 41.2).

3. Inhaling, draw in the belly and extend the arms in front of the chest. Open the hands while separating the arms and return the legs to their original straight position (Figure 41. 3).

4. Repeat steps 2 and 3 a total of 21 times, tensing and relaxing.

5. Finish with the concluding exercise (see Chapter 34).

Benefits: This will strengthen the arms, legs, knees, calves, shoulders, and all functions associated with the arms.

Note: This movement is similar to the fourth practice in the series, but in this practice the arms and legs are drawn in while tensing, strengthening the limbs.

CHAPTER 42

HOLDING AND RELEASING EFFORTLESSLY

FIGURE 42.1

FIGURE 42.2

FIGURE 42.3

FIGURE 42.4

FIGURE 42.5

FIGURE 42.6   FIGURE 42.7

Step-by-step instructional text

1. Place the feet shoulder width apart. Inhaling, draw in the belly and move the fists up and in toward the chest while lifting the toes (see Figures 42.1 and 42.2).

2. Exhaling, expand the belly out, extend the forearms forward and open the hands with palms facing up. At this time, also drop the toes back on the ground (Figure 42.3).

3. Repeat steps 1 and 2 a total of 21 times.

4. Finish the practice with the concluding exercise, *shougong*. With the palms facing up (Figure 42.4) lift the hands in front of the center of the chest (Figure 42.5). Turn the palms to face down (Figure 42.6) and relax them back to the sides of the body (Figure 42.7).

Benefits: This movement can strengthen the function of the kidneys, bladder, and prostate, as well as the health of the female reproductive organs.

Note: While practicing, keep the upper arms stationary.

CHAPTER 43

Earnest Exhortation

FIGURE 43.1

FIGURE 43.2

FIGURE 43.3

FIGURE 43.4

FIGURE 43.5

FIGURE 43.6   FIGURE 43.7

Step-by-step instructional text

1. Inhaling, raise both arms to the sides, elbows bent and raised. The shoulders are aligned like the seat of a mountain, palms facing forward with hands closed into fists. The soles of the feet are in contact with the ground (see Figure 43.1).

2. Exhaling, raise the heels (Figure 43.2), pushing the body upward. The fists open up, palms still facing forward (Figure 43.3).

3. Repeat steps 1 and 2 a total of 21 times.

4. Closing practice, *shougong*. Bring the hands up (Figure 43.4), palms facing upward, to the level of the *tanzhong* (Figure 43.5), then let them drop back down (Figure 43.6), placing them back in a relaxed manner to the sides of the body.

Benefits: Strengthens the kidneys and increases the ability of the lumbar vertebrae up to the upper thoracic vertebrae, including the arms and hands.

Note: The upper arms remain horizontal, without moving.

CHAPTER 44

REPENT AND BE SAVED

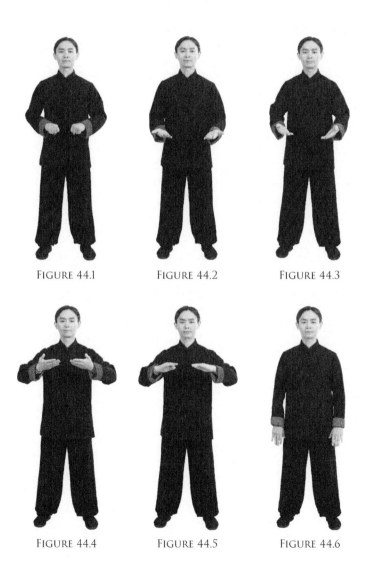

FIGURE 44.1   FIGURE 44.2   FIGURE 44.3

FIGURE 44.4   FIGURE 44.5   FIGURE 44.6

Step-by-step instructional text

1. With feet spread shoulder-width apart, raise the hands to the level of the *dantian*. Separated by about a fist's length, the "tiger's mouth" acupoints and thumbs of each hand should be directly facing one another, with the palms facing downward.

2. Inhaling, suck in the stomach, ball the hands into fists and tuck them in slightly toward the body (see Figure 44.1).

3. Exhaling, turn the hands over while opening the palms (Figure 44.2).

4. Repeat steps 2 and 3 for a total of 21 times.

5. Do the closing exercise, *shougong*. Raise the hands, palms up (Figure 44.3), until they are level with the *tanzhong* (Figure 44.4) before turning the palms over (Figure 44.5) and letting them fall slowly until they rest naturally at the sides (Figure 44.6).

Benefits: Can strengthen and extend the range of motion of elbows, wrists, and palms. Also strengthens the function of all organs in the area of the *dantian*.

Note: The focal point of this practice is on movement of the stomach.

CHAPTER 45

Echoing Back and Forth

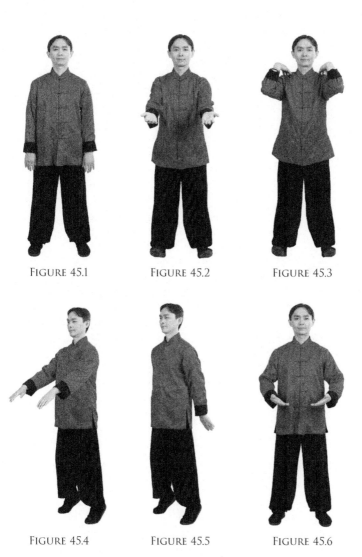

FIGURE 45.1   FIGURE 45.2   FIGURE 45.3

FIGURE 45.4   FIGURE 45.5   FIGURE 45.6

FIGURE 45.7   FIGURE 45.8

FIGURE 45.9   FIGURE 45.10

Step-by-step instructional text

1. Stand with feet shoulder-width apart, relax the entire body (see Figure 45.1).

2. As you inhale, swing both arms up to the shoulders and gently tap the shoulder region with the tip of the fingers. At the same time, lift the toes up (Figures 45.2 and 45.3).

3. As you exhale, swing both hands down, palms facing back, as the heels lift (Figures 45.4 and 45.5).

4. Repeat steps 2 and 3 a total of 21 times.

5. Finish with the closing exercise, *shougong*. Raise the hands, palms up (Figure 45.6), until they are level with the *tanzhong* (Figures 45.7) before turning the palms over (Figures 45.8 and 45.9) and finally letting them fall slowly until they rest naturally at the sides (Figure 45.10).

Benefits: This exercise lengthens and stretches the meridians, as well as relaxes the entire body by tapping the shoulders with the fingertips. It also strengthens all the areas along the meridians. This practice can also prevent high blood pressure, glycemia, and coronary diseases.

Inhaling, lift the toes.

Note: You only need to lightly tap the shoulder area with the fingers. The movement of the feet cannot be inverted.

Exhaling, lift the heels.

SECTION 3

養生九式 NINE STYLES FOR CULTIVATING HEALTH

CHAPTER 46

BASIC RELAXATION TECHNIQUE

Step-by-step instructional text

1. Stand straight with legs shoulder-width apart.

2. Imagine there is a thread coming through the body from the crown all the way down through the *huiyin*, and down to the floor between the legs. Imagine your entire body is like an airbag, thoroughly empty. In this way, relax the entire body.

3. From the tips of your hair all the way to the *yongquan* points, everything is empty and transparent as a crystal ball. In this way, tell yourself to relax.

4. Do this three times.

CHAPTER 47

PUSH ASIDE THE CLOUDS, SEE THE SUN

FIGURE 47.1   FIGURE 47.2   FIGURE 47.3

FIGURE 47.4   FIGURE 47.5

FIGURE 47.6

FIGURE 47.7

FIGURE 47.8

FIGURE 47.9

FIGURE 47.10

FIGURE 47.11   FIGURE 47.12   FIGURE 47.13

Step-by-step instructional text

1. Stand with the feet shoulder-width apart, relax the body from head to toe three times (see Figure 47.1).

2. After the body is relaxed, slowly overlap the hands with palms up and put them in front of the *dantian*. Inhale and imagine the *qi* is going into the *dantian* (Figure 47.2).

3. Exhale and raise the hands up along the body to the *tanzhong* (Figure 47.3).

4. Turn the palms facing up to the sky, feel as though you're lifting something with your hands, and lift the heels at the same time (Figure 47.4).

5. Slowly circle the arms outward, put the heels down (Figures 47.5–47.7).

6. Bring the hands back to the height of the *dantian* (Figure 47.8).

7. Repeat steps 2 to 6 a total of seven times. On the last repetition, bring the hands back to being overlapped with thumbs crossing in front of the *dantian* (Figure 47.9).

8. Closing exercise, *shougong*. With palms facing up, lift the hands up to the *tanzhong* (Figure 47.10). Turn the palms down (Figures 47.11–47.12) and place the hands back by the sides of the body (Figure 47.13).

Benefits: This posture is mainly for helping to lift us up and remove turbidity among the internal organs. In particular, those who have symptoms of poor blood circulation above the waist (such as issues with cervical vertebrae, chest, back) can benefit from this. People who often feel fatigued or dizzy, or have neuropathic pain in the head, shoulders, and arms can all try this posture.

CHAPTER 48

DISTRIBUTION OF THE *TAIJI*

FIGURE 48.1   FIGURE 48.2   FIGURE 48.3

FIGURE 48.4   FIGURE 48.5

FIGURE 48.6   FIGURE 48.7

FIGURE 48.8   FIGURE 48.9   FIGURE 48.10   FIGURE 48.11

Step-by-step instructional text

1. Stand with the feet shoulder-width apart, relax the body from head to toe three times (see Figure 48.1).

2. Squat slightly, slowly, making sure the knees do not go beyond the toes. The bottom of the palms are touching, with the ten fingers opening like a lotus. Imagine the hand

is holding a *taiji* ball (Figure 48.2) and inhale the *qi* into the *dantian*, then exhale the *qi* out from your nose, three times.

3. When inhaling for the fourth time, sink the *qi* into the *dantian*; when exhaling, imagine the *taiji* ball falling into the palm of the right hand. The right hand holds the *taiji* ball, moves, and extends to the right, and the head also rotates, eyes focusing on the *taiji* ball itself (Figures 48.3 and 48.4).

4. Inhale and move the *taiji* ball back to the center with the right hand (Figure 48.5)

5. Exhale and drop the ball into the palm of the left hand. Hold the *taiji* ball in the left hand and extend out the left hand. Turn the head to the left; eyes on the *taiji* ball (Figure 48.6).

6. Repeat the previous step, then bring the *taiji* ball back to the center (Figure 48.7).

7. Repeat steps 3 to 6 seven times, then get up and stand in the original position.

8. Do the closing exercise, *shougong*. With the palms facing up (Figure 48.8), lift the hands to the *tanzhong* (Figure 48.9). Turn the palms down (Figure 48.10) and place the hands back by the sides (Figure 48.11).

Benefits: This exercise can improve concentration, solve problems related to the cervical vertebrae, head and eyes, and also increase lung capacity and adjust bronchial-related problems. The action of forcing the five fingers open can help improve blood circulation, such as when one's hands and feet get cold or numb in the winter; peripheral nerve circulation will also benefit.

Note: When doing the movement, the waist should be relaxed and straight, and so should the spine. When inhaling and exhaling, let the chest stretch out. Straighten your shoulders and focus your attention on your hands. When the palms are slowly pushed out, the five fingers should be stretched out.

CHAPTER 49

TOUCHING HEAVEN AND EARTH

FIGURE 49.1   FIGURE 49.2   FIGURE 49.3

FIGURE 49.4   FIGURE 49.5   FIGURE 49.6

Step-by-step instructional text

1. Place the feet shoulder-width apart. Relax from head to toes three times (see Figure 49.1).

2. When you breathe in, the fingers of the hands should face each other, with the palms facing upward, as you raise them evenly up to the *tanzhong* (Figure 49.2).

3. As you breathe out, the palm of the right hand faces upward with the fingers pointed inward toward the body, press the hand toward the sky; the palm of the left hand faces downward, with the fingers pointed in toward the body, use force to press the hand toward the ground (Figures 49.3 and 49.4). While you are performing this movement, the upward and downward pushing action will stretch and pull the vertebrae, one by one, up toward the nape of the neck and the *dazhui*.

4. As you breathe in, the two hands return toward the *tanzhong* (Figures 49.4 and Figure 49.5).

5. When you breathe out, the palms switch directions: the left palm faces toward the sky while the right hand pushes toward the ground (Figure 49.6).

6. Continue in this fashion: breathe in as the two hands return toward the *tanzhong*, and breathe out as you push the hands away from each other. Repeat the exercise a total of 21 times.

7. Closing exercise, *shougong* (see Chapter 48).

Benefits: Practicing this exercise often, will make it harder to develop bone spurs, and will benefit the natural curvature of the spine. You are strengthening the elbows, wrists, fingers of both hands, and the joints of the arms. The practice improves circulation, prevents blockages of the *qi* and blood in the arms, and is helpful if any of the above-mentioned areas have discomfort.

Dazhui point: Located on the nape of the neck. If you look downward (tilting your head), one of the cervical vertebrae on the back of the neck will stick out; under this bone is a sunken area—this is the *dazhui*.

CHAPTER 50

FLIPPING THE SPIRIT TURTLE

FIGURE 50.1   FIGURE 50.2   FIGURE 50.3

FIGURE 50.4   FIGURE 50.5   FIGURE 50.6

FIGURE 50.7   FIGURE 50.8   FIGURE 50.9

Step-by-step instructional text

1. Stand with the feet shoulder-width apart, relax three times from head to toe (see Figure 50.1).

2. Place the hands on the hips with thumbs facing forward (Figure 50.2). Exhaling, squat down (Figure 50.3); inhaling, straighten the legs. Repeat three times.

3. Inhaling, slightly squat and rotate the upper body to the right moving only from above the waist. Tuck in the chin putting pressure on the carotid arteries and rotate the head with the upper body looking toward the upper back (Figure 50.4).

4. Exhaling, slowly rotate the body back to center (Figure 50.5).

5. Inhaling, using the same method, rotate to the left (Figure 50.6).

6. Exhale and rotate back to the front (Figure 50.5).

7. Repeat steps 3 to 6 a total of 21 times.

8. Concluding practice, *shougong*. Raise the hands (Figure 50.7), palms facing up, to the level of the *tanzhong*. Turn the hands over (Figure 50.8) and lower them back to the sides of the body (Figure 50.9).

Benefits: This practice is helpful for the digestive system, (particularly in countering) gas, excessive acidity, and poor peristalsis. If the practice increases the production of saliva, separate it into three parts, and swallow it to the *dantian*: the exercise stimulates the secretion of beneficial enzymes.

Note: The inhalation should incorporate a movement of drawing the lower belly in while gently lifting the perineum.

CHAPTER 51

A Pair of Dragons Spitting Pearls

FIGURE 51.1   FIGURE 51.2   FIGURE 51.3

FIGURE 51.4   FIGURE 51.5   FIGURE 51.6

FIGURE 51.7   FIGURE 51.8   FIGURE 51.9

Step-by-step instructional text

1. Stand with feet shoulder-width apart. Relax from head to toe three times. Using the simple relaxation methods, adjust the breath. With the palms of the hands facing up, bring the hands up in front of the chest, imagining you are holding a large balloon (see Figure 51.1).

2. Inhaling, forcefully curl the fingers into fists (Figure 51.2).

3. Exhaling, slowly bend the knees and lower the fists (Figure 51.3).

4. Extend the fists forward. Just before reaching full extension, forcefully open the hands pointing the fingers up. Imagine sending the balloon out, and focus on straightening the spine (Figure 51.4).

5. Inhaling, turn the hands over and curl the fingers into fists, with the palms facing up, and gently pull the hands back (Figure 51.5) as you come back to standing (Figure 51.6).

6. Repeat movements 3 to 5 a total of seven times.

7. Concluding practice, *shougong*. With the palms facing up (Figure 51.7), lift the hands to the level of the *tanzhong*, at the center of the chest (Figure 51.8). Turn the palms down and lower the arms back to the sides (Figure 51.9).

Benefits: This practice can prevent dementia and strengthen the knees and lower back. It improves circulation of blood and *qi* throughout the body, improves the peripheral nervous system, and the immune system. It can also slow the deterioration and prevent stiffness of the limbs, while nourishing the organs and exercising the waist, hips, spine, and legs.

CHAPTER 52

Nod Your Head and Wag Your Tail

FIGURE 52.1

FIGURE 52.2

FIGURE 52.3

FIGURE 52.4

FIGURE 52.5

Step-by-step instructional text

1. Place the feet shoulder-width apart and relax the whole body from head to toe three times.

2. Adjust the breath until it becomes natural. Stand naturally, arms relaxed to the sides. Imagine the whole spine becoming empty and relaxed. In particular, imagine the arms being light and relaxed like those of a child's rattle drum (see Figure 52.1).

3. Twist the body from the waist up, allowing the arms to alternately swing to the front and to the back. When the left hand slaps into the right shoulder, the right hand should slap into the lower back, in the area of the left kidney (Figures 52.2–52.4).

4. When the right hand hits the left shoulder, the left hand should hit the area of the right kidney. Rotate the body in unison with the neck (Figure 52.5).

5. Repeat movements 3 and 4 a total of seven times.

6. Practice the concluding exercise, *shougong* (see Chapter 51).

Benefits: This practice strengthens the kidneys and lower back. It can help ease stiffness and back pain from frequent and long periods of sitting. It is also helpful for stuck shoulder syndrome, stiff hands and legs, as well as numbness in the upper extremities.

CHAPTER 53

Tense All, Relax All

FIGURE 53.1   FIGURE 53.2   FIGURE 53.3

FIGURE 53.4   FIGURE 53.5

Step-by-step instructional text

1. Placing the feet shoulder-width apart, relax the whole body from head to toe three times.

2. Extend the arms to the sides (see Figure 53.1).

3. Inhaling, make fists with both hands while slowly bringing both hands to the front, crossing the arms. At the same time relax the body while slightly bending the knees, moving as slowly as possible (Figure 53.2).

4. Continue squatting all the way to the ground, reaching the hips back as if squatting on a toilet (Figure 53.3).

5. Exhaling, relax the hands, relax the body and slowly stand up to the original position (Figures 53.4 and 53.5).

6. Repeat movements 2 to 5 a total of seven times.

7. Practice the concluding exercise, *shougong* (see Chapter 51).

Benefits: This practice prevents the musculature of the body from aging and deteriorating, and the bones from developing osteoporosis. It also collects the mind and spirit, preventing them from becoming dispersed, and helps the kidneys, back, and the musculoskeletal system as a whole. *This form is NOT suitable for those with blood pressure issues or cardiovascular pathologies.*

Note: In the process of squatting down and standing up, the body should be completely relaxed, one should not use force.

CHAPTER 54

THE CHILD WORSHIPPING THE BUDDHA

FIGURE 54.1   FIGURE 54.2   FIGURE 54.3

FIGURE 54.4   FIGURE 54.5   FIGURE 54.6

Step-by-step instructional text

1. Stand with feet shoulder-width apart. Relax from head to toe three times (see Figure 54.1).

2. Place the palms together in front of the chest. Inhaling, keeping the palms together, extend both arms up over the head, stretching up as high as possible (Figures 54.2 and 54.3).

3. Exhaling, without bending the knees, bend forward at the waist lowering the hands to touch the ground between the feet (Figures 54.4 and 54.5).

4. Inhaling, slowly come back up (Figure 54.6).

5. Repeat steps 2 to 4 a total of 21 times.

6. Concluding exercise, *shougong* (see Chapter 51).

Benefits: This form stretches and relaxes the important joints of the body, preventing stiffening, deterioration, and atrophy; it also promotes cardiovascular circulation, and boosts the immune system.

CHAPTER 55

CULTIVATING THE KIDNEYS

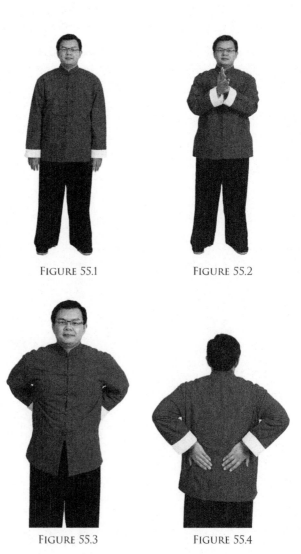

FIGURE 55.1

FIGURE 55.2

FIGURE 55.3

FIGURE 55.4

Step-by-step instructional text

1. With the feet shoulder-width apart, relax the whole body from head to toe and adjust the breathing until it becomes natural (see Figure 55.1).

2. Forcefully open the hands, and imagine a blazing hot sun in each palm. Clap and rub the hands together vigorously (Figure 55.2).

3. After the palms become heated from the friction, place them over the kidneys, on the lower back (Figure 55.3).

4. Massage the area making complete circles with the palms, 36 times. Maintain natural breathing (Figure 55.4).

5. Concluding practice, *shougong* (see Chapter 51).

Benefits: Aids kidney function and guards against problems arising there, such as bladder and urinary tract dysfunctions.

奇經八脈簡易通脈功法
SIMPLIFIED EXERCISES TO OPEN UP THE EIGHT EXTRAORDINARY MERIDIANS

CHAPTER 56

PREPARATORY VISUALIZATIONS

FIGURE 56.1   FIGURE 56.2

Step-by-step instructional text

1. Relax the whole body while standing, with feet shoulder-width apart. Let the hands naturally hang down, palms relaxed and facing behind you.

2. From the hair on the top of the head downward, visualize each body part relaxing completely, until it disappears: the head, down past the face to the chest, the back, hips, between the legs, all the way down to the *yongquan* points on the bottom of the feet. Repeat the relaxation process three times.

3. Visualize the whole body as an air sac, completely empty. There is a string running down the body's central axis, from the *baihui* on the apex of the head to the *huiyin*, then continuing all the way (to the floor) in between the feet.

Inhale and exhale three times. When inhaling, visualize the air-sac-body completely deflating; when exhaling, visualize the body expanding back to its original form. At this time, just breathe naturally.

4. Visualize eggs, roughly the size of chicken eggs, under the *yongquan* points on the bottom of the feet. Those who tend to have high blood pressure can visualize the eggs as dark (black, grey, blue), and those who tend to have relatively weaker/lower *qi* and blood can visualize the eggs as white. These are not real eggs of any substance, just the empty shells. By creating the feeling of treading on thin ice, the mind state is that of being scared to break the shells. One can visualize walking on the surface of water or on cotton, or have the feeling of standing high up in the clouds, floating in space.

Benefits: This preparation style helps the body relax thoroughly; this is a preparatory step to the simplified exercises to open up the eight extraordinary meridians.

Note: How to check whether you're completely relaxed? Briefly feel whether your palms are ever so slightly warm, numb, and swollen. If there are no such indications, exert a small amount of force from the palm to open up the fingers (on both hands), then relax and repeat in this way three times until relaxed.

Note: The goal of doing this visualization exercise is to help clear out any *qi* blockages or stagnant *qi* from the body. Perform the preparatory exercise in order to practice well.

Note: This visualization exercise helps the body relax and "disappear." The preparatory practice allows later practices to be performed in an even better manner.

CHAPTER 57

PREPARATORY EXERCISES

FIGURE 57.1   FIGURE 57.2   FIGURE 57.3

FIGURE 57.4   FIGURE 57.5

Step-by-step instructional text

1. Relax the whole body while standing, feet shoulder-width apart, and let the hands hang naturally with palms facing behind you (see Figure 57.1).

2. Inhale and slowly raise the hands with palms facing up (Figure 57.2).

3. Slowly raise the hands to the center of the chest, by the *tanzhong* (Figure 57.3).

4. Exhale, turn the palms face down (Figure 57.4).

5. Slowly move hands back down (Figure 57.5).

6. Repeat steps 2 to 5 a total of three times.

Benefits: This exercise can help return *qi* to its original state and make the breath more uniform.

CHAPTER 58

RETURN *QI* TO ITS ORIGINAL STATE

FIGURE 58.1   FIGURE 58.2   FIGURE 58.3

FIGURE 58.4   FIGURE 58.5   FIGURE 58.6

FIGURE 58.7   FIGURE 58.8   FIGURE 58.9

FIGURE 58.10   FIGURE 58.11   FIGURE 58.12

Step-by-step instructional text

1. Relax the whole body while standing, feet shoulder-width apart, and let the hands hang naturally with palms facing behind you (see Figure 58.1).

2. Inhaling, bend the knees slowly without going past the toes (Figure 58.2).

3. Bend backward at the waist while extending the arms to the side (Figure 58.3).

4. Move the arms back and up, as if drawing a big circle, as if holding a big ball, with the back slightly arched back (Figure 58.4).

5. The arms circle back down in the front, slowly, as if wanting to give the body a hug (Figure 58.5).

6. The hands come back to about two fists-width in front of the *dantian*; pause there for a few seconds, and breathe naturally. The entire sequence should be done with the feeling of holding a balloon. The attention should be put on the balloon itself (Figure 58.6).

7. Inhaling, draw the belly in, as if to touch the spine; exhaling, stick out the belly and visualize the balloon returning to where the hands are, in front of the *dantian* (Figure 58.7).

8. Repeat steps 2 to 7 for 7 or 21 times.

9. Concluding exercise, *shougong*. With palms facing up (Figure 58.8), raise the hands to the level of the *tanzhong* in the center of the chest (Figure 58.9).

10. Turn the palms down (Figures 58.10 and 58.11) and bring the arms back to rest at the sides of the body (Figure 58.12).

Note: While doing this exercise, place your tongue gently on the roof of the mouth, behind the top teeth, as you inhale. Exhaling, place the tongue at the root of the bottom teeth. When your mouth is filled with saliva, swallow it in three small gulps. This can nourish the *dantian*.

Benefits: Aids blood circulation and improves the functionality of the limbs and spine. The antioxidant nature of the exercise helps to avoid premature aging, slowing down the aging process. It also frees up the pathways of the eight extraordinary meridians, while strengthening the root and cultivating the spirit.

Note: The fingers face each other with about one-fist distance in between. There should be a distance of two fists between the stomach and the palms.

CHAPTER 59

UNSTOPPABLE

FIGURE 59.1 FIGURE 59.2 FIGURE 59.3

FIGURE 59.4 FIGURE 59.5 FIGURE 59.6

Step-by-step instructional text

1. Relax the whole body while standing, feet shoulder-width apart, let the hands hang naturally with palms facing behind you (see Figure 59.1).

2. Inhaling, bend the knees slowly with palms facing upward (Figure 59.2).

3. Slowly raise the hands level with the *tanzhong* at the center of the chest (Figure 59.3).

4. Exhaling, stand back up slowly while turning the palms outward and placing the attention on the *laogong* acupoints on both hands. Extend the hands and open the palms forcibly while exhaling completely. Focus on the fingertips and visualize all impure *qi* (inside the body) turning into black smoke, and being dispelled through the *laogong* points on both hands (Figures 59.4 and 59.5).

5. Inhaling, slowly bend the knees, palms facing the chest, and visualize all the pure *qi* from sky and earth being absorbed into the body (Figure 59.6).

6. Repeat steps 4 to 5 a total of 21 times

7. Concluding exercise, *shougong* (see Chapter 58).

> Benefits: Practicing this exercise during your meditation and *daoyin* routines helps keep your thoracic cavity, lungs and bronchi, the lung meridian, and heart in good shape. It can relieve discomfort in the chest and overall *qi* stagnation. It also has a beneficial effect on opening the meridians on the arms.

CHAPTER 60

VANQUISHING DRAGONS AND TIGERS

FIGURE 60.1

FIGURE 60.2

FIGURE 60.3

FIGURE 60.4

FIGURE 60.5

FIGURE 60.6

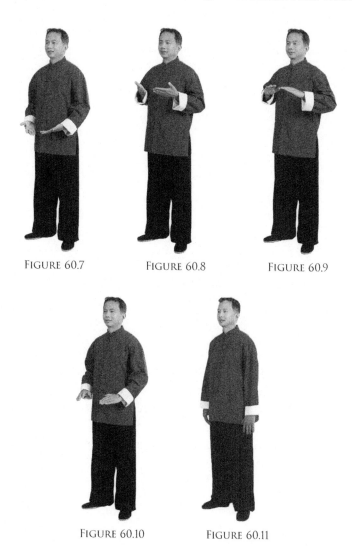

FIGURE 60.7   FIGURE 60.8   FIGURE 60.9

FIGURE 60.10   FIGURE 60.11

Step-by-step instructional text

1. Relax the whole body while standing, feet shoulder-width apart, let the hands hang naturally with palms facing behind you (see Figure 60.1).

2. Step forward with the left foot, placing 30 percent of the body weight onto it and 70 percent on the right foot in the

back; keep the center of gravity over the right foot. The tailbone is directly over the right heel. Begin in the position of holding a ball with the left hand above and the right hand below (Figure 60.2).

3. Extend the left arm forward and pull the right hand back next to the right ear. Maintain this posture and focus the eyes on the angle made by the thumb and index finger of the left hand.

4. Inhale, draw the belly in and lift the anus. Open the eyes wide and tense the ten fingers. The tongue should be at the roof of the mouth, behind the top teeth (Figure 60.3).

5. Close the eyes and exhale, expanding the belly outward and relaxing the anus (Figure 60.4).

6. Repeat steps 4 and 5, maintaining the same breathing pattern, and repeat 21 times.

7. Switch sides. With the right foot in front and the left at the back, begin in the position of holding a ball (Figure 60.5). Extend the right arm forward and pull the left hand back to the left ear. Maintain this posture and focus the eyes on the angle made by the thumb and index finger of the right hand (Figure 60.6). Repeat the breathing instructions in steps 4 and 5, 21 times.

8. Concluding exercise, *shougong*. Turn the palms up (Figure 60.7) and raise them to the level of the *tanzhong* at the center of the chest (Figure 60.8).

9. Turn the palms down (Figures 60.9 and 60.10) and relax the hands back to the sides of the body (Figure 60.11).

Benefits: This practice benefits the arms, hips, waist, eyes, spine, and one's attention span.

CHAPTER 61

DIRECTING WATER UPWARD

FIGURE 61.1   FIGURE 61.2   FIGURE 61.3

FIGURE 61.4   FIGURE 61.5   FIGURE 61.6

FIGURE 61.7   FIGURE 61.8   FIGURE 61.9

FIGURE 61.10   FIGURE 61.11   FIGURE 61.12

Figure 61.13   Figure 61.14   Figure 61.15

Figure 61.16   Figure 61.17   Figure 61.18

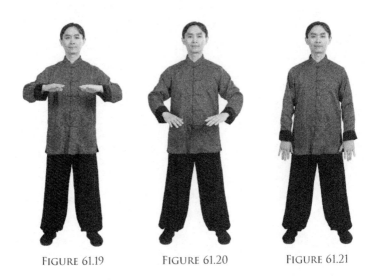

FIGURE 61.19   FIGURE 61.20   FIGURE 61.21

Step-by-step instructional text

1. Relax the whole body while standing, feet shoulder-width apart, let the hands hang naturally with palms facing behind you (see Figure 61.1).

2. Cross the hands with palms facing up and the thumbs out to the sides (Figure 61.2).

3. From their place at the *dantian*, raise the arms up on the inhale (Figure 61.3). When they reach the level of the *tanzhong* in the middle of the chest, turn the palms over and exhale (Figures 61.4 and 61.5). Repeat this action three times.

4. Inhale, the hands make a sword shape (Figure 61.6). Bend the body forward at the waist without bending the knees (Figure 61.7). Try your best to touch the ground with the fingers (Figure 61.8).

5. Exhale and stand back up straight, draw the hands up against the body from the *dantian* to the *tanzhong* at the center of the chest (Figure 61.9). Point the fingers up (Figure 61.10).

6. Extend the sword fingers to the sides, focusing the *qi* on the fingertips. Extending the arms to the sides, exhale completely (Figure 61.11).

7. Again, bend at the waist, attempting to touch the fingers to the ground (Figures 61.12 and 61.13).

8. Exhale and stand back up straight, draw the hands up against the body from the *dantian* to the center of the chest (Figures 61.14 and 61.15).

9. Extend the sword fingers out in front of the chest, focusing the *qi* there, stretching the arms out as far as possible, and exhale completely (Figure 61.16). Repeat steps 7 to 9, 21 times.

10. Concluding exercise, *shougong*. The palms of the hands are facing up (Figure 61.17). Lift the arms level with the center of the chest (Figure 61.18).

11. Turn the palms down (Figures 61.19 and 61.20). Relax the arms back to the sides of the body (Figure 61.21).

Benefits: Can improve osteoporosis, weakness of the waist and knees, kidney water deficiency, soreness of the waist and back, as well as prevent bone spurs, strengthen the legs, and prevent premature aging. It can also help open the channels of the back and benefit the spine, arteries, and veins.

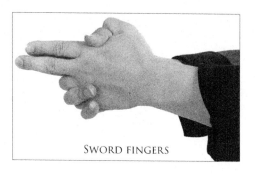

SWORD FINGERS

CHAPTER 62

HUGE BEAR TURNS ITS BODY

FIGURE 62.1 FIGURE 62.2 FIGURE 62.3

FIGURE 62.4 FIGURE 62.5 FIGURE 62.6

FIGURE 62.7   FIGURE 62.8   FIGURE 62.9

FIGURE 62.10   FIGURE 62.11

Step-by-step instructional text

1. Relax the whole body while standing, feet shoulder-width apart, let the hands hang naturally with palms facing behind you (see Figure 62.1).

2. Clap the hands together and rub them until hot. Place both hands on the kidney region and rub 36 times (Figures 62.2 and 62.3).

3. Inhale and rotate the upper body to the right. As you do this, press the chin down to put pressure on the two throat arteries and turn the head along with the body (Figure 62.4). Open the eyes as wide as possible and look as far back to the right as you can.

4. Exhale and slowly come back to the original central position. Stop there for a moment (Figure 62.5). Continue pressing the chin downward as you do so.

5. Inhale once more and rotate the upper body to the left. Turn the head along with the body (Figure 62.6). Open the eyes as wide as possible and look as far back to the left as you can.

6. Exhale and slowly come back to the original position in the center (Figure 62.5).

7. Repeat steps 3 to 6 for a total of 21 times.

8. Concluding exercise, *shougong*. With the palms of the hands facing up (Figure 62.7), lift the arms level with the center of the chest (Figure 62.8).

9. Turn the palms down (Figure 62.9 and 62.10), relax the arms back to the sides of the body (Figure 62.11).

Benefits: This practice style is good for the head, eyes, shoulders, neck, kidneys, spine, and waist.

CHAPTER 63

COMPLETELY OPENING THE EIGHT MERIDIANS

FIGURE 63.1   FIGURE 63.2   FIGURE 63.3

FIGURE 63.4   FIGURE 63.5   FIGURE 63.6

FIGURE 63.7   FIGURE 63.8   FIGURE 63.9

FIGURE 63.10   FIGURE 63.11

Step-by-step instructional text

1. Relax the whole body while standing, feet shoulder-width apart, let the hands hang naturally with palms facing behind you (see Figure 63.1).

2. Inhale and raise the hands up, palms facing up (Figure 63.2).

3. When the hands reach the *tanzhong*, turn the palms over, facing downward (Figures 63.3 and 63.4).

4. Continue to raise the hands up until you reach the crown of the head (Figure 63.5), then let the palms naturally hang downward (Figure 63.6).

5. Exhale and let the hands slowly make their way down, past the nostrils, then the *tanzhong*, to finally reach the *dantian* (Figure 63.7).

6. Repeat steps 2 to 5 a total of three times.

7. On the fourth inhale, bring the hands up and raise the heels. When the hands have reached the crown, induce trembling in your body. Both arms and hands should also tremble (Figures 63.8 and 63.9). While you are trembling, continue breathing naturally.

8. When you have trembled to the point you want to come down, exhale, and slowly let the hands come down. The heels then slowly come back to the ground (Figures 63.10 and 63.11).

9. Repeat steps 7 and 8 for a total of 21 times.

10. Concluding practice, *shougong* (refer to Chapter 62).

Benefits: This movement can completely clear up all the blocked *qi* in the eight extraordinary meridians. It also helps to open up all the joints, clearing all obstructions in the four limbs, while strengthening joints and bones of the arms and legs.

CONCLUDING PRACTICES

All concluding practices finish in the same way. That is, when you have completed the motions of the exercise you were doing, walk in place until your breath has returned to the state it was in before you started your practice.

CHAPTER 64

CONCLUDING PRACTICE I

FIGURE 64.1

FIGURE 64.2

FIGURE 64.3

FIGURE 64.4

FIGURE 64.5

FIGURE 64.6

FIGURE 64.7

FIGURE 64.8

FIGURE 64.9

FIGURE 64.10

FIGURE 64.11

FIGURE 64.12

FIGURE 64.13   FIGURE 64.14   FIGURE 64.15

FIGURE 64.16   FIGURE 64.17   FIGURE 64.18

FIGURE 64.19   FIGURE 64.20   FIGURE 64.21

Step-by-step instructional text

1. Stand straight and relaxed with feet shoulder-width apart and hands naturally dropped by the sides (see Figure 64.1).

2. Inhale and bring the hands up, palms facing upward. When you reach the *tanzhong* in the center of the chest, turn the palms down, breathe out and slowly let the hands come down (Figures 64.2–64.4). Repeat this motion three times.

3. On the third repetition, when the palms reach the *tanzhong* and face downward, begin bringing the hands down and, following their motion, bend the body forward at the waist. As the palms face back, straighten the arms out behind the body (Figure 64.5).

4. Once you have bent to your maximum capacity (Figure 64.6), begin exhaling and bring the body back up (Figure 64.7).

5. As you stand, continue extending the arms up and back, and arch the upper body toward the back, according to your capacity (Figure 64.8).

6. Keeping the arms straight, inhale once more, bend the

upper body forward again and bring the arms back behind the body (Figures 64.9 and 64.10).

7. Exhale once more, bring the body back up and then arch backward again (Figures 64.7 and 64.8).

8. Continue inhaling and exhaling, repeating the sequence above seven times.

9. Come back to the initial position and stand there until the whole body is relaxed (Figure 64.11).

10. Inhale, palms of the hands facing up (Figure 64.12), and lift the arms level with the *tanzhong* at the center of the chest (Figure 64.13).

11. Exhale, palms facing downward (Figure 64.14), and squat down (Figure 64.15) until the tip of the fingers touch the ground (Figure 64.16).

12. Inhale and rise slowly with palms facing each other (Figure 64.17); continue slowly bringing the hands up until they go past the head (Figure 64.18).

13. Exhale and slowly bring the hands down to the *dantian* (Figures 64.19 and 64.20). Finally, relax both hands to the sides of the body (Figure 64.21).

Concluding exercises are practiced after your moving or sitting practice; they aim to clear away the blocked *qi* clogged up in the muscles and bones, and to allow the *qi* and breath to return to their original, neutral state.

CHAPTER 65

CONCLUDING PRACTICE II

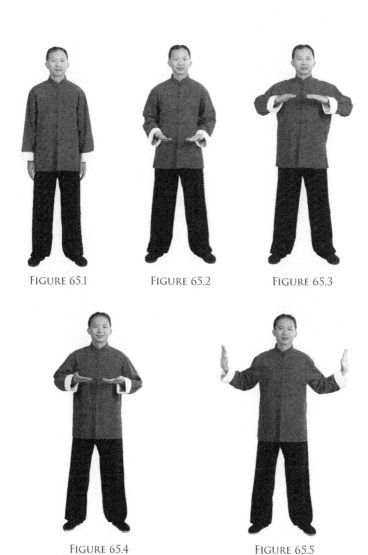

FIGURE 65.1   FIGURE 65.2   FIGURE 65.3

FIGURE 65.4   FIGURE 65.5

Figure 65.6

Figure 65.7

Figure 65.8

Figure 65.9

Figure 65.10

FIGURE 65.11   FIGURE 65.12   FIGURE 65.13

FIGURE 65.14   FIGURE 65.15   FIGURE 65.16

FIGURE 65.17   FIGURE 65.18

Step-by-step instructional text

1. Relax the entire body in a standing position, with the feet shoulder-width apart and the hands naturally hanging to the sides (see Figure 65.1).

2. Breathe in. With the palms facing upward, slowly raise the hands up to the height of the *tanzhong* point on the chest. Turn the palms over as you breathe out and gradually lower the hands back down (Figures 65.2 and 65.3). Repeat this three times.

3. As you breathe in, the hands gradually come back up to the *tanzhong* (Figure 65.4), as you breathe out, the palms face to the left and right as you extend the arms outward to the sides. Very naturally stretch and extend the chest out as well (Figures 65.5 and 65.6).

4. As you breathe in, the head naturally hangs down as the hands come back in to the *tanzhong* point. Visualize that you are breathing in all of the best, purest air available on Earth (Figures 65.7–65.9)

5. As you breathe out, the hands again face to the left and the

right and push outward, extending the arms. The chest naturally extends and stretches out. Visualize that all of the impure *qi* of the body is expelled out (Figures 65.10 and 65.11). Repeat steps 4 and 5 a total of seven times.

6. After the seventh time, as you breathe out, slowly squat down (Figure 65.12); as you reach the bottom of your squat, the fingers touch the ground (Figure 65.13).

7. As you breathe back in, the body slowly stands back up (Figure 65.14). The palms face each other and slowly rise above the head (Figure 65.15).

8. As you breathe out, the hands slowly lower to the *dantian* area (Figures 65.16 and 65.17), then relax back down to the sides of the body (Figure 65.18).

CHAPTER 66

CONCLUDING PRACTICE III

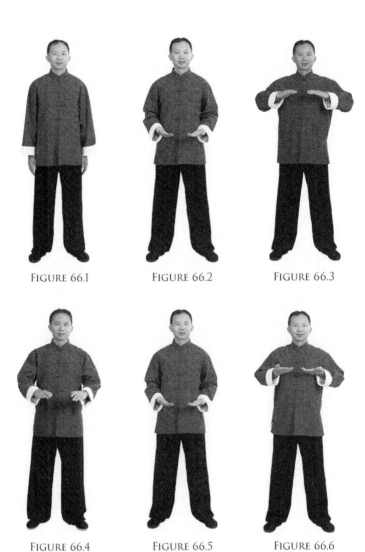

FIGURE 66.1   FIGURE 66.2   FIGURE 66.3

FIGURE 66.4   FIGURE 66.5   FIGURE 66.6

FIGURE 66.7

FIGURE 66.8

FIGURE 66.9

FIGURE 66.10

FIGURE 66.11

FIGURE 66.12

FIGURE 66.13   FIGURE 66.14   FIGURE 66.15

FIGURE 66.16   FIGURE 66.17

FIGURE 66.18

FIGURE 66.19

FIGURE 66.20

FIGURE 66.21

FIGURE 66.22

FIGURE 66.23

FIGURE 66.24

FIGURE 66.25   FIGURE 66.26   FIGURE 66.27

Step-by-step instructional text

1. Relax the entire body in a standing position, with the feet shoulder-width apart and the hands naturally hanging to the sides (Figure 66.1).

2. Breathe in. With the palms facing upward, slowly raise the hands up to the height of the *tanzhong* point on the chest. Turn the palms over as you breathe out and gradually lower the hands back down (Figures 66.2–66.4). Repeat this three times.

3. As you breathe in, the hands gradually come back up to the *tanzhong* (Figures 66.5 and 66.6).

4. Turn the palms over as you breathe out, then bend at the waist as you bring the hands down to the ground (Figures 66.7–66.9).

5. As you breathe in, the fingers face each other, imagine that both hands are holding buckets of water or holding bricks— you should have a general feeling of force being applied in the hands. Gradually bring the hands up to the *tanzhong* point (Figures 66.10–66.12).

6. The hands rotate with palms facing upward as you extend them upward. The arms straighten up to the sky with palms facing up (Figures 66.13 and 66.14).

7. As you breathe out, the arms open up to the sides and slowly lower (Figure 66.15).

8. Bend the body over as the hands reach down to the ground once again (Figures 66.16 and 66. 17).

9. Breathe in again, and repeat steps 5 to 8 a total of seven times.

10. Breathe in with palms up (Figure 66.18), as the hands rise from the height of the *dantian* up to the *tanzhong* point on the chest (Figure 66.19).

11. As you breathe out, turn the palms over and begin to squat down (Figure 66.20), bring the hands down as well, so that the fingers touch the ground (Figures 66.21 and 66.22).

12. Breathe in as the body gradually comes back up (Figure 66.23); with palms facing each other, slowly raise the hands above the head (Figure 66.24).

13. As you breathe out, the hands again slowly lower down to the *dantian* (Figures 66.25 and 66.26). Relax and bring the hands back to the sides (Figure 66.27).

CHAPTER 67

CONCLUDING PRACTICE IV

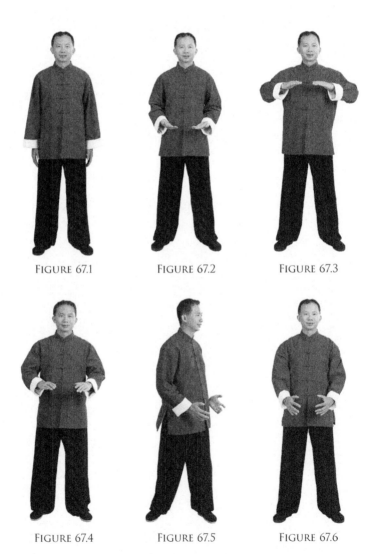

FIGURE 67.1   FIGURE 67.2   FIGURE 67.3

FIGURE 67.4   FIGURE 67.5   FIGURE 67.6

FIGURE 67.7

FIGURE 67.8

FIGURE 67.9

FIGURE 67.10

FIGURE 67.11

FIGURE 67.12

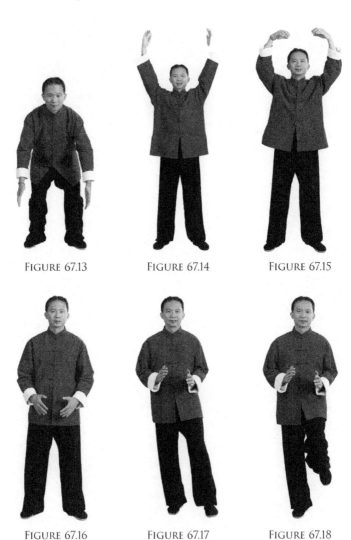

FIGURE 67.13   FIGURE 67.14   FIGURE 67.15

FIGURE 67.16   FIGURE 67.17   FIGURE 67.18

FIGURE 67.19   FIGURE 67.20   FIGURE 67.21

Step-by-step instructional text

1. Relax the entire body in a standing position, with feet shoulder-width apart and the hands naturally hanging to the sides (see Figure 67.1).

2. Breathe in. With the palms facing upward, slowly raise the hands up to the height of the *tanzhong* point on the chest. Turn the palms over as you breathe out and gradually lower the hands back down. Repeat this three times (Figures 67.2–67.4).

3. The hands are placed in front of the *dantian*, as if you were holding a ball (Figure 67.6).

4. As you breathe in, the upper body turns to the right. After you have turned the body fully, breathe out (Figure 67.7).

5. As you breathe in, the upper body returns to the starting position. Breathe out (Figure 67.6).

6. Breathe in again as the upper body turns to the left. After you have turned it fully, breathe out (Figure 67.5).

7. Breathe in once again, and return the body back to the starting position. Breathe out (Figure 67.6).

8. As you breathe in, the palms face up and the hands move from in front of the *dantian* up toward the *tanzhong* in the center of the chest. As you breathe out, the palms turn downward and the hands move back down (Figures 67.8–67.10).

9. Squat down, bring the fingers down to touch the ground (Figures 67.11 and 67.12).

10. Breathe in, slowly bringing the body back up (Figure 67.13).

11. With palms facing each other, slowly bring the hands over the head (Figure 67.14).

12. As you breathe out, the hands gradually go back down to the *dantian* area (Figures 67.15 and 67.16).

13. The hands stop in front of the *dantian* (Figure 67.19). Take the left foot, slightly raise it up and then give a soft kick downward (Figures 67.17 and 67.18)

14. Return the left foot back to the standing position (Figure 67.19), then switch to the right foot and do the same thing: slightly raise it up and then give a soft kick downward (Figures 67.20 and 67.21).

15. Bring the right foot back to the starting position, hands resting by the sides, completing the exercise.

Printed in Great Britain
by Amazon